The Boiseans: At Home

By Arthur A. Hart

Historic Boise, Incorporated

Historic Boise, Incorporated
Boise, Idaho

Third Printing 1992

Historic Boise, Incorporated, is a non-profit organization dedicated to the preparation and publication of works on the history, architecture, and culture of Boise, Idaho. Proceeds from the sale of this book will be used to publish future titles in the series.

Printed by Joslyn & Morris, Incorporated.

Photographs are from the collection of the Idaho State Historical Society.

Library of Congress Catalog Card No. 84-082012

TABLE OF CONTENTS

1.
Cover photograph: The Moore-Cunningham house at the corner of Warm Springs Avenue and Walnut Street was built by C.W. Moore in 1891.

To Novella Dee

FOREWORD

In *Historic Boise* we outlined briefly the city's architectural history from 1863 until 1938. This volume is a collection of short essays that attempt to capture the flavor of the life and times of some of the families which played a significant part in the city's history. As such, it deals more with biography than with architecture; but few things reflect the aspirations of a people so well as do the homes they build for themselves.

To own a fine house is a mark of success, and Boiseans of earlier times were no different from those of today in recognizing this. They built as well as the circumstances permitted, not only to show off their own hard-won prosperity but often with the consciousness that they were enhancing the beauty of the little city they had helped grow from a dusty crossroads in the sagebrush.

This book is admittedly tilted heavily in the direction of the well-known and the successful among Boise's early citizens. For every family represented here there were hundreds who lived in more modest houses, worked hard for a decent living for their families, and kept their names out of the papers.

My earnest effort has been to seek out the stories of the most interesting of Boise's early leaders, and to select those who also built homes representative of the city's passing architectural parade.

Whenever possible I have tried to shed light on the lives of Boise's pioneer women; but as everyone who studies the sources knows, women were a neglected minority in earlier histories. There were many subscription histories devoted to the lives of Idaho men, but only rarely did women rate more than brief mention as wives and mothers. In the 1860s and 1870s women made the newspapers when they married, gave birth, or died. It was well into the 1880s before social notes began to appear, and not until the 1890s was there a "Society" section in the paper. As valuable as these sources are as indicators of how Boiseans entertained themselves, it is hard to find in them the personal touches that could make women's lives more real.

Written accounts by Boise women describing their lives in the 19th century are rare. We have been able to discover a few and to include them as written. Although these somewhat redress the imbalance inherent in the subscription biographies, most present life from the point of view of women in Boise's social elite. They do not reveal the lives or experience of women whose lot was harder and who rarely wrote about it. Oral histories, collected in the past 20 years provide useful information about Boise women who did not leave written records of their lives.

Here then are the Boiseans at home. It has been great fun getting to know them.

Arthur A. Hart
Boise, Idaho 1984

The Boiseans about whom this book is written were men and women prominent in the life of their city. They were pioneers of Idaho who shared a common dream — to establish new lives in a wild and undeveloped land and to improve their fortunes. Almost without exception they succeeded. Those who did not make a lot of money were successes in other ways — they achieved positions of respect because of their contributions of talent and leadership that made Boise City a better place to live.

The Boiseans were a cosmopolitan lot. They came from many lands and from states of North and South, both during and after the Civil War. On a stroll down Main Street you could hear conversations in a variety of accents — English, Irish, German, Scandinavian, and Spanish. There were the more exotic sounds of Chinese, and on occasion Shoshoni or Paiute.

Many of the men you saw on the street had worn the uniform of the Confederate States of America — about as many as had worn the blue of the Union. Most of the Southerners were Democrats — enough of them to swing the Territory's early elections their way. But in city politics, at least, there was little real partisanship. It was the man that counted. The city's first mayor was an Englishman, and two others from those early years were born in Germany.

The frontier army post next to the city was manned in large measure by immigrants from Ireland and Germany. Fort Boise's most popular commandant was a German who served in the Indian Wars and was active in the city's social life for many years thereafter. Some of Boise's business leaders had also fought Indians in the West before the Civil War. They volunteered again in the 1870s when the Nez Perces, Bannocks, and Sheepeaters rebelled against white encroachment on their lands.

Boise City became the capital of Idaho Territory in 1864, succeeding Lewiston, which held the honor only a year. Idaho's population had shifted from north to south in response to new gold discoveries in Boise Basin (1862) and the Owyhee Mountains (1863). A feature of Boise life thereafter was the gathering of the territorial legislature and its official and unofficial activities.

Governors of territories were appointed (usually for reasons of politics rather than competence) by the President of the United States. Idaho, like other sparsely populated Western outposts, was a victim of the "spoils system" in that most of these political appointees were largely ignorant of Western concerns and of frontier life. Blessedly, several didn't bother to come to Idaho even after accepting the appointment. Of those who did, a few were capable and conscientious, some were barely competent, and at least one was both an eccentric and a crook. In the post-Civil War era it is perhaps not surprising that three of Idaho's territorial governors had been generals in the Union army.

Their importance in this account is the part they played in the city's social life, for they were often present in the homes of the Boiseans of whom we write.

The varied social activities in early Boise are a reflection both of the times and of the backgrounds of the people. This has always been a club town, where it was possible to join or start a group in pursuit of almost any interest. The Germans were leaders in forming a number of social clubs featuring athletics, singing, and good lager beer made by local brewers — all Germans. During the Franco-Prussian war they collected a large purse to be sent to the old country for the relief of widows and orphans. (As late as 1906, when they dedicated their new Turn Verein building at Sixth and Main, they sang "Die Wacht Am Rhein" before giving three cheers for Teddy Roosevelt.)

2.
A Whist Club was popular in Boise at the turn of the century. Laura Moore Cunningham is the woman standing in the center of this group of card players.

2

In the years covered by our account Boise had an Irish Fenian Brotherhood, a Scottish Caledonian Club, a German Harmonie Society, and a New England Society. There were groups devoted to various athletic interests, including the Jockey Club, Gentlemen's Driving Club, Boise Athletic Club, German-American Athletic Association, Polo Club, Rod and Gun Club, Pasttime Club (devoted to bicycling), and eventually Boise Country Club. People with cultural interests could join the Dickens Club, Holland Literary Circle, Columbian Club, Bonne Heure Society, Philharmonic, or a number of amateur theatrical groups.

In addition to the churches and their circles, there were the Women's Christian Temperance Union, Boise Prohibition Club, Salvation Army, and Jesuit-sponsored Pioneer Educational Society. Countering the forces of reform was a Liquor Dealers Protective Association. Other groups, organized to promote occupations or business interests, included agricultural societies, the Idaho Poultry and Pet Stock Association, a lumber dealer's group with the euphonious name of Concatination of Hoo-hoos, Idaho State Horticultural Society, State Beekeepers Association, and Idaho Mining Exchange. Doctors, dentists, pharmacists, attorneys, and osteopaths were all organized into professional societies of their own, with social activities involving their wives.

The volunteer fire department, which at one time or another between its founding in 1876 and the forming of a professional force in 1902 had enrolled most of Boise's prominent men, was a social group of great importance. The wives were as active as their husbands in organizing regular dances and supper parties. The old firemen continued to march in parades long after they were no longer called upon to fight fires.

Fraternal organizations were important in the lives of Boiseans, and women's auxiliaries provided much social activity. Masons, Odd Fellows, and Knights of Pythias were pioneer groups in the city. Patriotic organizations included the Grand Army of the Republic for Union veterans and the Daughters of the American Revolution.

A woman who grew up in 19th-century Boise was asked by a relative in the east to describe the hardships of pioneer women. Leona Hailey Cartee, daughter of John Hailey, and daughter-in-law of Lafayette Cartee, remembered only "the joys of life" in Boise for those in her family's circle of friends:

"As I think of those dear women in the early Seventies it seems to me they were happy and life was not so hard. Money was plentiful, nearly everyone that I knew had a Chinese cook, and usually he was not only the cook but general house boy — washing, ironing, and doing all the heavy work. For those who could not afford Chinese help there were always squaws who were glad to do the washing and hard work."

Young Leona Hailey obviously led a happy and sheltered life not typical of all Boise women of her day. She had little worry about family finances, although her hard-working father would certainly have told a different story about a period that saw the nationwide Panic of 1873 and the failure of the Bank of California in 1875. Both had far-reaching financial impact on Idaho business. John Hailey suffered severe losses during the Indian wars later in the decade when his stagecoach line was repeatedly forced to suspend operations because of attacks or the threat of raids on his stations and his horses.

Calling Boise "the dearest little city I have known in all of my wanderings," Leona described Grove Street as "the prettiest street in Boise, and rightly named, for the entire residence section on one side, along the dirt sidewalk, was shaded by towering poplars. These were the first trees — later they were replaced with more lasting trees. On the opposite side of the street the 'Big Ditch' as we children called it, flowed swiftly, while picturesque water wheels groaned and droned as they lifted water from the stream and sent it on the way into the little irrigating ditches...

"Grove Street was a picture of quiet restful life. In fact, there seemed to be a general impression that to live on Grove Street and belong to the Episcopal church was all that was necessary to open the doors of good society and unbar the gates of heaven."

In Leona Hailey Cartee's reminiscence of her mother's friends in little old Boise City of the 1870s, only positive adjectives appear. They were "cheery, bright, charming, entertaining, cultured, brilliant, beautiful, sweet, or gentle... lovely women striving always for the highest and best, and especially helpful to the young people." Those must indeed have seemed "the good old days" and Boise City a sagebrush branch of heaven.

3.
Grove Street had reached its zenith in the 1890s when this picture was taken. Frank and Irene Coffin's house at Eleventh and Grove is at left.

The little brick house on Grove Street, just west of Sixth, is as historic as any in Boise. It was built in 1864 by Cyrus and Mary Elizabeth Jacobs less than a year after the town was founded. They had come from Oregon in March, 1863, with daughters Edith and Fannie and Cyrus' brother Simon. When the townsite was platted in July, 1863, Cy Jacobs acquired six lots and opened a general merchandise business in a tent at Seventh and Main.

In 1852 young Jacobs had passed the site of Boise on his way to Oregon in an emigrant wagon. Neither he nor the tens of thousands of other pioneers who followed the Oregon Trail along the bench south of Boise River ever imagined that a city would someday grow beside the tree-lined river below them. He certainly never dreamed that he would spend most of his life there.

In Oregon Cy Jacobs met and married the attractive daughter of General Joel Palmer, a prominent pioneer who had served as Speaker of the House of Representatives, Superintendant of Indian Affairs, and a Major General of Volunteers in the Indian Wars of the 1850s.

The word that best described Cyrus Jacobs was "enterprising," and the Idaho Tri-weekly Statesman used it regularly in listing his remarkable achievements. Jacobs built a gristmill where he ground farmers' grain for a share of the crop. He used this to make sour mash from which he distilled a potent rye whisky marketed in the mining camps as "Jacobs' Best." The mash residue was then used to fatten hogs. "Keep your money at home and give employment to home labor" urged Jacobs, in newspaper ads featuring his manufacture of bacon, hams, shoulders, lard, flour, corn meal, graham flour, cracked wheat and bran. "I also manufacture a very fine article of liquors and vinegar, wash tubs, butter firkins and general cooperage," he noted, and promised dealers better prices than they could get by importing.

In addition to the fine brick store he built at Seventh and Main in 1865, Jacobs put up a stone storage building behind his house on Grove Street that is still standing.

Mary Elizabeth Jacobs had five children — four daughters and a son. Two of the girls died young. The boy, born in 1878, was christened Alexander Palmer, but went by A. Palmer Jacobs as a man, using his mother's family name.

The Jacobs house was a popular gathering place, small as it seems today. This delightful glimpse, from the Statesman of January 12, 1871, suggests that Mary Elizabeth and Cyrus were generous hosts: "Sixteen of our city belles, all unmarried, and sixteen of our gallant beaux, raided last Tuesday evening upon the quiet abode of Mr. Cy. Jacobs, and took possession . . . As usually happens among the gay and happy of the opposite sexes under the like circumstances, they forthwith proceeded to improvise a dance, and 'chased the hours with flying feet' until three o'clock in the morning." Since none of the Jacobs children were old enough to be part of this group, it seems likely

4.
Cyrus Jacobs was a man of many accomplishments. He pioneered manufacturing in Idaho.

5.
The Cyrus Jacobs' house on Grove near Sixth is the city's oldest brick house. Mary Elizabeth, son Palmer, and Cyrus Jacobs are shown in this photograph made in about 1870.

6.
Mary Elizabeth Jacobs was the daughter of noted Oregon pioneer General Joel Palmer.

that Charlie Himrod, a clerk in the Jacobs store, who boarded with them, instigated the merry invasion. (Both Cyrus Jacobs and Charles Himrod would serve terms as mayor of Boise City later)

The Jacobs circle of pioneer friends included William J. McConnell, elected Governor of Idaho in 1892. In April, 1895, McConnell presented the hand of his daughter Mamie to William E. Borah in a quiet wedding ceremony performed in the Jacobs' parlor.

7.
Thomas E. Logan served Boise City first as its postmaster. He was elected mayor four times in the 1870s.

8.
The 1865 adobe house of Mayor and Mrs. Thomas E. Logan has been moved to the Idaho Historical Society's Pioneer Village in Julia Davis Park.

Mr. and Mrs. Thomas E. Logan arrived in Boise City by covered wagon on September 2, 1864. Just before their arrival they lost their infant daughter — a sad beginning to a new life in Idaho. They also had a two-year-old son, Leonard.

Logan went into partnership with Gustave Billicke in a general merchandise business on Main Street. In 1865 they erected one of the city's first brick store buildings, and for the next quarter century Logan was one of Boise's best-known business and civic leaders. He was appointed postmaster by President Grant in 1869 and elected mayor four times in the Seventies.

The Logans bought an adobe house on Sixth Street south of Main in the late Sixties and lived there until 1892 when they moved into a new mansion in the north end. The Logan adobe, a rare building type in the Pacific Northwest, was moved to Julia Davis Park in 1971 by the Idaho Historical Society after it was threatened with demolition. Restoration and furnishing with antiques from the 1870s was accomplished with help from the Idaho Historical Auxiliary, Miller Foundation, and Sons and Daughters of Idaho Pioneers. Dr. Eugene B. Chaffee, president emeritus of Boise State University, led a successful fund raising campaign to preserve the historic house.

Few Boiseans were aware that the Logan house was made of sun-dried mud bricks, since it was painted soon after it was built. This preserved it against the destructive forces of rain and weathering that turn most adobe buildings back into earth in a few years, especially in northern latitudes. Although pale green in 1971, research revealed that the house was first painted brick red — the color it wears today.

The Logan house was the scene of many lively social occasions through the years. The passing parade of famous visitors who were entertained there included governors, generals, and federal officials from Washington. The pages of the Tri-weekly Statesman afford delightful glimpses of events that brought people to see Mayor and Mrs. Logan:

In June, 1889, a steady stream of callers came and went, "the principal motive of their visit being to see a beautiful specimen of the night-blooming cereus which had opened its golden petals and displayed its magnificent white blossom on the balmy evening air that came in through the parlor windows."

On New Year's day, 1892, as on so many other such days, the Logan house "was besieged during the afternoon and evening hours by an army of callers . . . Those who called were warmly welcomed and delightfully entertained. From the center of the parlor ceiling a wreath of holly, in lieu of mistletoe, was suspended. As it is leap year and the usual order of events is reversed, the young men, including Governor Willey, made valiant efforts to stand beneath the green circle; but the rush was so great that all were disappointed."

Most of the houses on Warm Springs Avenue are included in a National Register historic district. Nearly all of them stand on what was once the homestead of George Whitfield Russell. Happily, the Russell farmhouse still stands where it did in 1868, although few people passing by have any idea it is that old.

Russell built the two story house at 1035 Warm Springs Avenue shortly after he and his family settled on a homestead that included most of what is now called the East End. Russell's property extended from the Cottonwood Creek flume to where the Natatorium later stood, and from Boise River to the foothills.

In its present state the style of the Russell house appears to be Greek Revival — a not implausible diagnosis since neo-classicism was still in vogue in the 1860s. However, a recently discovered photograph (right) shows that it was originally Italianate, with a front porch of exceptional elegance. Jig-sawed "gingerbread" made this structure as lacy as an old valentine. There was also a tiny "widow's walk" of similar ornate character topping the hipped roof. Some typical features of Italianate architecture, such as the brackets under the eaves, were removed when the house was remodeled into its present form.

When George Russell married Mary Baird in Peoria, Illinois on December 2, 1856, he had already had his share of adventures in the far West. In 1849 he had sailed around Cape Horn to California, later returning by way of the Isthmus of Panama to the family farm in Illinois.

Russell was especially proud of his horses, and during the presidential campaign of 1860 had the honor of driving candidate Abraham Lincoln in a parade behind his finest team. This was a moment he never forgot.

In 1862 the Russells joined a large wagon train headed for Oregon. They drove the same horses that had pulled Lincoln and, according to Russell, they were the finest animals in the entire caravan. Their party camped on the bench south of Boise River the summer before the army established a fort at the foot of the hills and a town was laid out nearby. The family was barely settled near Salem when news that gold had been discovered in Boise Basin reached Oregon. Russell went to The Dalles with a pack train, and began hauling supplies to the mines in Idaho.

He brought his family to Boise in August, 1864. The town, which hadn't been there when they passed by in 1862, was already the capital of Idaho Territory. George Russell bought an interest in a hotel and moved his family into it. Shortly after, he acquired the Halfway House on the road to Idaho City and they moved again. Finally, in 1868, the Russells homesteaded the Warm Springs Avenue property where they stayed the rest of their lives.

George and Mary Russell raised five children on the prosperous ranch east of Boise — then a mile out of town. There were two boys and

9.
G.W. Russell's elegant Italianate house looked like this in about 1890. Today it has a classical porch and has lost its Victorian "gingerbread".

10.
Elliott's 1884 History of Idaho Territory *included this lithograph of the Russell homestead. It shows the spacious acres of the Russell farm before there were any near neighbors on what became Warm Springs Avenue.*

9

three girls. Elizabeth, the oldest daughter, was married to Robert Sidebotham in the house at 1035 Warm Springs in 1878. After George and Mary died (1901 and 1902), the Sidebothams continued to live there for many years — long enough to see the dirt road that passed the homestead become Warm Springs Avenue and a fashionable residential neighborhood.

10

RESIDENCE OF G.W. RUSSELL, EAST BOISE AVENUE BOISE CITY. I.T.

11

Many of Boise City's leading citizens in the 19th century were born in one of the small German kingdoms, principalities or dukedoms that existed prior to Bismarck's unification of the empire in 1871.

The European revolutions of 1848, perennial warfare, and nearly universal military conscription led thousands of Germans to emigrate to the New World in the decade that followed. John Lemp, born at Niederweisel, Hesse-Darmstadt in 1838, was one of these. In 1852, aged 14, he sailed for America to seek his fortune.

The Pike's Peak gold rush brought Lemp west in 1859, and after a few years of unsuccessful prospecting in Colorado he joined a small band of adventurers headed for Idaho. He arrived in Boise on July 8, 1863 — one day after the town's founding fathers had met in a log cabin to plat the future capital.

After a short stay in Idaho City (then called West Bannack) John Lemp returned to Boise and bought a fledgling brewery, recently started by a character later remembered only as "Whistling Pete." The price was a teacup full of gold dust. The year was 1864, and that summer Boise City was made capital of the year-old Territory of Idaho.

Lemp's Boise Brewery flourished, and by judicious investment, good management, and consistently generous support of public causes he was soon the most popular man in town. In a few years he was the richest.

In 1865 Catherine Kohlepp and her family arrived in Boise by covered wagon. They, like John Lemp, were Hessians. He met and married her that same year. The Lemps produced one of the town's largest families, in an age of large families. Their 13 children included twins Ida and Ada, named for their native state and county.

John Lemp's personal popularity is reflected in the many honors paid him and in frequent notices in the papers. In 1870 the German community organized a Turn Verein and Harmonia Society. Lemp was elected president. In 1875 he was elected mayor.

The growing Lemp family led him to enlarge his wooden frame house on Grove street in 1874, but even before the work was completed he decided to tear up the plans and build on a substantially grander scale. By then there were five little Lemps, and Catherine was expecting the twins.

The house was nearly complete at Christmas, 1874, when it was described as "perhaps the finest finished dwelling in the Territory." German carpenters meticulously crafted a large entry hall, parlor, dining room, kitchen, pantry, a bath and ten bedrooms! The Lemps obviously looked forward to a lot more children. There was also a

11.
John Lemp: a poor German lad who made good in the new world of Idaho.

12.
The Gothic Revival Lemp cottage on Grove Street had 10 bedrooms, none too many for 13 children and hired help.

13.
The Lemp twins, Ada and Ida.

summer kitchen and wash house 14x20 feet — another necessity of a large household. A reporter who visited the new Lemp house was especially impressed by the hand-grained wood, gilt wallpaper, and Mr. and Mrs. Lemp's bedroom, which he called "splendid."

John and Catherine Lemp's son Herbert, born in 1885, was elected Boise mayor in 1927. He was the only son of a mayor to be elected to the post, but died of injuries received in a polo accident only four days after taking the oath of office.

When William H. Nye died in March, 1894, he was one of the city's best known pioneer business men. His Grove Street house was the most charming Gothic Revival cottage in a row that included those of Lafayette Cartee and John Lemp.

Nye had come to Boise after serving with distinction in the Civil War. He had personally organized the first volunteer company of the Seventh Massachusetts Infantry and served as its captain. He served with that unit in the Army of the Potomac, and was present at the battle of the Antietam in September, 1862. Poor health led to his discharge soon after.

Nye, a native of Boston, had worked there as a druggist before the war. When he came to the raw frontier town of Boise City in 1865 he again took up the trade. He worked for others until 1869 when he was able to form W.H. Nye & Co. In 1875 he bought the brick building at the northeast corner of Eighth and Main that he had been renting and continued in business at that location until his retirement in the late Eighties. "Nye's Corner" was considered the most valuable retail location in the city, and was later purchased by Nathan Falk as the site for the big new store built in 1896.

By 1880 William and Caroline Nye had three daughters, Emily, Elizabeth and Edith. A son was born in 1882. The couple had cultural interests and took part in the activities of such groups as The Holland Literary Circle. Nye was also fond of chess, and his drugstore was a center "where the good players love to congregate. Mr. Nye has the reputation of being the champion," observed the Statesman. His toughest competition was said to be D.P.B. Pride, Territorial Secretary and Register of the U.S. Land Office. "Alphabetical Pride" also served as Territorial Attorney General in the Eighties.

The reputation of Grove Street as the city's finest residential area in the Seventies and Eighties was enhanced by small gems like the Nye house. Its profusion of wooden "gingerbread" gave distinction to an otherwise modest dwelling. When Elliott's History of Idaho Territory was published in 1884, this was one of the homes pictured. It was also singled out as recently as 1975 for inclusion in Oregon Historical Society's history of Pacific Northwest architecture, "Space, Style, and Structure", as an example of the "cottage orne," and is the most richly decorated of all the examples chosen to illustrate the Gothic Revival style. The Nye house burned to the ground on September 30, 1908.

14.
William H. Nye's drug store at Eighth and Main.

15.
The Nye cottage, like the Lemps', was Gothic Revival, but a lot more ornate.

15

16

"General Cartee's grounds and improvements surpass anything this side of California," said an 1872 newspaper account describing the lush vegetation and handsome buildings at Fourth and Grove streets. Lafayette Cartee was proprietor of the Grove Street Nursery and also Idaho Territory's Surveyor General. He was a civil engineer by training.

More than to any other citizen, Boise City in the 1870s owed its oasis-like character to Cartee. He took the lead in importing many kinds of shade, ornamental and fruit trees for his nursery, and stocked a wide variety of berries and floral species. The General's buildings were designed with style, reflecting the ideas of Andrew Jackson Downing, who, in a number of influential books, had persuaded Americans to live in rural villas with verdant tree-shaded grounds.

The popular and respected General Lafayette Cartee had known his share of personal tragedy. In 1862, while working as engineer and supervisor of Oregon Steam Navigation Company's railway project around the Dalles of the Columbia River, his young wife Mary died leaving him with four children. Carrie was 5, Ella 3, Ross 1, and baby Mary Bell only a few months old.

Cartee moved his little family back to the Willamette valley where his wife's sister-in-law Henrietta Bell, came to take care of them while he went to Idaho alone to follow his engineering work. In 1863 he was in Rocky Bar, and in 1866 was appointed Surveyor General of Idaho Territory with offices in Boise. His letters to his children in Milwaukie, Oregon at this time are tender and filled with longing for the time when he can bring them to Boise. He urges them to be good and to study hard in school. He tells his little boy that he has bought him a pony and can hardly wait for him to ride it.

The house at Fourth and Grove that Cartee built for his family was a lively place. In addition to the children there were Aunt Henrietta, her brother Darius, and Allen Thompson and Peter Bell, civil engineers who worked in the Surveyor's office. The children grew up with loving attention and many of the pleasures that small town life in Idaho afforded. They had pets, including a dog named "Watch." They took summer excursions into the mountains with their father and his friends. In August, 1871, the Cartees, C.W. Moores and Donaldsons took a trip "to luxuriate on game and trout," as the paper put it.

Lafayette Cartee never remarried. His dignified bearing and kindly manner masked a trace of sadness that never left him. It did not prevent him from being personally popular and widely respected in all community matters. He was regularly elected chairman of committees dedicated to the betterment of Boise City, including one to form a fire department and another to secure a railroad. Earlier, in Oregon, he had been elected to the legislature soon after his arrival in 1850. In 1854 and 1855 he served as Speaker of the House, and was chief clerk in the Surveyor General's office.

16.
Lafayette Cartee was one of Boise City's most talented and respected pioneers.

17.
The Cartee house on Grove Street was long considered one of Boise's showplaces. Lafayette Cartee's lush nursery, orchard and grounds made it even more so.

18.
Mary Bell Cartee was youngest of the General's children.

The Cartee children received the best education their father could arrange. He sent oldest daughter Carrie to Europe in 1875 to study music and languages at Mannheim, Germany. He bought her a magnificent grand piano as a present when she returned — an instrument now in the Idaho Historical Museum. Ella Cartee studied in San Francisco for two years. She had a fine singing voice and played the guitar. Son Ross had artistic talent, especially in drawing. He became a civil engineer like his father but was also an architect of ability.

The Cartee house was a Boise showplace, singled out for praise in several early publications. Lithographic views of the Gothic Revival structure appeared in Portland's West Shore magazine in October, 1878, and in Elliott's History of Idaho Territory in 1884. It was torn down in 1952.

19

As owner, editor, and publisher of the Idaho Tri-weekly Statesman from 1871 until 1889, Judge Milton Kelly had wide renown and influence in the young territory. He was noted for scathing editorial opinions, and enjoyed nothing more than a good fight with political opponents.

An 1899 subscription biography used moderate language to describe Kelly's editorial style: "His opinions were his own and were given with such candor and courage that they commanded the respect of the people." By today's standards they were often outrageously intemperate and insulting. Small wonder that Kelly was the constant target of equally course and abusive language, or that on one occasion he was assaulted on the street, stabbed, and beaten by a man who took exception to his comments.

Milton Kelly and his wife Lois were already middle aged when they arrived in Idaho in 1862. They had met and married in Ohio in 1843 and already had three daughters and a son when they emigrated west. They settled first in Boise Basin, and when Idaho became a territory in 1863, attorney Kelly was elected to the first legislature. Although defeated for re-election in 1864, Kelly received what may have been Abraham Lincoln's last political appointment, signed shortly before he was shot in Ford's Theater on April 14, 1865. Kelly's term as justice of the territorial Supreme Court lasted until 1870. It was during this period that political opponents dubbed him "Bribery Kelly" because of a controversial decision he had made in a case involving mine ownership at Silver City.

Although Kelly was entirely innocent of the charge, his enemies brought it up for as long as he lived — reason enough to make him bitter and violent in his editorial reactions. Readers of territorial newspapers were treated to many a feud and Kelly was usually in the middle of them. His chief opponents were "Old Hill" of the Owyhee Avalanche and Thomas J. Sutton of the Idaho World. The language got so foul that some sensitive readers canceled their subscriptions.

The only known view of Milton and Lois Kelly's house is the one published in Elliott's 1884 History of Idaho Territory. It shows it to have been a gabled Italianate structure with a prominent two-story bay window. A feature of Elliott's lithograph is the row of Lombardy poplar trees along the street in front of the house. Since the tall, graceful Lombardies were fast growing they were planted everywhere in early Boise. The Kelly house stood on Idaho Street, exact location unknown.

Milton Kelly was 71 when he retired as Statesman publisher in 1889. His wife Lois was 68. They moved to a ranch east of the city acquired some years earlier when Kelly had bought the hot springs resort east

19.
Judge Milton Kelly wielded the wickedest pen in Idaho Territory as editor and publisher of the Tri-weekly Statesman.

20.
Elliott's 1884 History of Idaho Territory *contained this quaint lithographic view of the Kelly house. The San Francisco artist who drew the picture on lithographic stone worked from a photograph and added stock figures to give his scene some life.*

20

of Table Rock. Boise people had been going there since the 1860s. The Kellys spent their last years improving the property — as it turned out, all in vain. The springs went dry a few years after hot wells were developed on the other side of Table Rock.

The Kelly daughters married prominent Boise citizens. Ellen was Mrs. James H. Bush; Kate became Mrs. Joseph Perrault, and Anna married Edgar Sencerbox.

Jimmy Hart was one of Boise City's popular and jovial citizens. He was married to an attractive and amiable woman who shared his talent for making friends. Since he ran a saloon on Boise's Main Street, this was a valuable asset, but Jimmy's great talent was his flair for humor in advertising.

Through the years, James H. Hart had more than his share of newspaper coverage, achieved by regularly getting his advertising messages into the news columns. Jimmy had something amusing to say about every important current event, and found a reason for a special celebration at his saloon for every one of them.

In 1881 he wrote a letter to the editor of the Idaho Tri-weekly Statesman begging that he not be confused with a well-known Mormon bishop — also named James H. Hart. Since Bishop Hart served in the territorial legislature at the time, the people of Boise certainly knew the difference, but it gave Jimmy a wonderful chance to tell his own story:

"It keeps me pretty lively to take care of one wife and live. I used to be a type sticker; worked in the New York Tribune office in 1865, served my time as an apprentice at the printing business, corner of Ann and Nassau streets in 1849 . . . am now making drunkards."

In 1880 Hart described his life as a saloon keeper. He had tended bar in Orofino, Placerville, and Boise, "but has given up the idea of getting rich selling whisky alone, and therefore caters to the taste of everyone — keeps on hand 'eatables as well as drinkables,' dry goods, wet goods, and general merchandise."

For years Jimmy Hart's "eatables" included a locally famous clam chowder. He dispensed it every Friday, free to his customers. On other nights he featured "Jimmy Hart's famous baked beans."

Jimmy's home life also made the papers, in ways that suggested a happy and rewarding relationship among members of the growing Hart family. James Hart and Eliza Paynton were married in New York City on November 5, 1866. In a few years four of her brothers also came to Boise City. The warmth of the Hart household is communicated in this account of May, 1875:

"On last Saturday thirty-four young fairies, aged from three years to about ten, assembled at Jimmy Hart's on Grove Street to celebrate Miss Minnie Hart's sixth birthday. And indeed what more glorious time to celebrate the birth of the young than the season when buds are opening and blossoms coming forth and birds singing love songs in the trees. And these young cherubs made the air musical with their turtling and cooing, and their voices rang lounder and sweeter than the birds in the budding branches. Mrs. Hart had a table spread with all sorts of delicacies which the young so much love . . ."

21.
Pioneer artist Charles Ostner sketched this view of Jimmy Hart's modest home for his 1878 lithograph of Boise. The house, which no longer stands, was much like that of Richard C. Adelmann which has been preserved in Julia Davis Park.

22.
James H. Hart at a reunion of pioneers.

23.
Jimmy Hart's saloon, also from Ostner's 1878 lithograph.

21

22

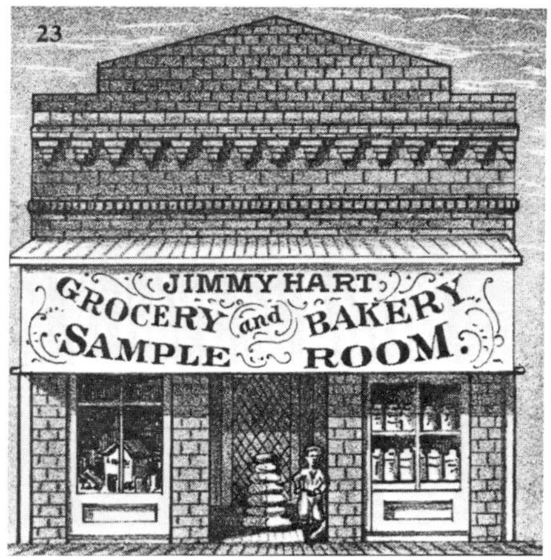

23

"Blessings on thee Minnie and your little friends. Thou art the fairest, most modest, and sweetest breathed of all the flowers of Idaho."

The modest little house on Grove Street was also the scene of a happy party in 1876 when Jimmy and Eliza celebrated their tenth wedding anniversary. Happily, they lived to accept the warm affection of many friends on their Fiftieth in 1916. Their three daughters and two sons were with them.

James, Jr. was a volunteer fireman like his father and like him served as Chief in the volunteer department. He was a tinsmith by profession.

Jimmy Hart, Sr. did much to help little old Boise keep its sense of humor in good times and bad. He died at 88 on April 25, 1925.

It was gold that brought fifteen-year-old James Pinney to the far west with his father in 1850. They mined in California for a year until lured to Oregon in 1853 by news of other gold strikes. In 1857, after several years of running pack trains to the mines, Pinney returned to the midwest to visit his parents in Iowa. In 1859 the Pike's Peak gold rush in Colorado again drew him westward.

1862 found Pinney again operating a pack string, this time to the gold regions of Idaho. He operated in such famous camps as Elk City, Orofino, Florence, and Auburn, Oregon. In 1863 he opened a store in Bannack City in Boise Basin, only to be burned out the next year. In 1864 Abraham Lincoln appointed him postmaster and he opened a book and stationery business. But again fire struck Bannack (now renamed Idaho City) and again he started over.

James Pinney was reappointed postmaster at Idaho City in 1868, and in July, 1869 his wife Mary died at only 25. Her grave, enclosed by the ornate cast iron fence he brought from his native Ohio later that year, can still be seen in the old Idaho City cemetery.

Pinney opened the City Book Store on Boise's Main Street in 1869 as a branch of his Idaho City business. He commuted between the two towns until 1873 when he moved to Boise and married Mary A. Rogers. He built her a house "on the west side of the public square," which the newspaper called "a mansion." By the standards of that time, it was. Portland's West Shore magazine published a lithographic view of it in 1878 that shows it to have been a two-story hip-roofed Italianate house with a cupola.

Pinney's property, on the block bounded by Eighth and Ninth and Jefferson and State, was the site of the stylish Columbia Theater he opened in 1893. The corner nearest Eighth and Jefferson became Columbia Park.

Even before he was elected to the first of five terms as Mayor of Boise City in 1881, Pinney had made his mark in the capital city. In 1876 the Statesman described him as "one of Idaho's best and most beloved pioneers." His store, where he sold toys, bird cages, cigars and tobacco, stationery, periodicals, pocket cutlery, fishing tackle, playing cards, and even apples in season, prospered. Musical instruments and sheet music would be added later. The Statesman called it a "mammoth bookstore," and it even sold books.

James Pinney had loved the theater ever since his youth in Ohio. When Peter Sonna built an opera house on the second floor of his hardware store at Ninth and Main, he hired Pinney to be his booking agent and manager. In April, 1892 Pinney began planning a theater of his own. He hired German-born Montana architect John C. Paulsen to design an Elizabethan-style playhouse for the Jefferson Street property. Pinney was more than busy without the new venture, since he was mayor of the city, still had the bookstore, and was a member of both the School Board and Board of Trade.

24.
James A. Pinney, long-time mayor, bookseller and theatrical promoter.

25.
The Pinneys' Italianate house stood on Eighth Street across from the first Central School.

26.
This Pinney family portrait included the mayor's parents from Ohio.

James and Mary Pinney had a daughter Annis. In 1902 she was working as a stenographer for attorney William E. Borah when Walter Mendenhall proposed marriage. She was a June bride in the just finished St. Michael's cathedral at Eighth and State, across the street from her parents house. Mendenhall managed the new Pinney Theater, built in 1908 across from the old Columbia, for many years after James Pinney died in 1914.

In September, 1891, shortly before the C.W. Moores moved to the big new mansion then being built on Warm Springs Avenue, an elegant reception was held in their home at Eighth and Grove for the ladies of The Women's Christian Temperance Union. The Statesman called the occasion "a social event," and described the Moore house on Grove Street as "palatial."

"The house was beautifully decorated with flowers and the lady hostess and her accomplished daughters appeared at their best" said the reporter. The mansard-roofed Moore house had been considered the territory's finest dwelling since its completion by banker C.W. Moore in 1879. It was a three-story brick house with a fashionable French look new to Idaho. The mansard roof was topped with lacy cast iron cresting, and 50 scroll-cut wooden brackets supported the eaves. Two bay windows, also finished off with iron cresting, gave sculptural form to the house and extended the entry hall and front parlor. The interior woodwork, imported from the midwest, included a solid walnut newel post and ornate balustrade on the staircase, and a spindled portiere above the hall. Pocket doors eight feet tall made it possible to treat the front parlor and dining room as one room or two. Most of these details were salvaged by the Idaho Historical Society in 1971, just before the house was demolished by urban renewal, and can be seen in historical interiors at the State Museum in Julia Davis Park.

The flavor of social life in The Nineties in Boise can be felt in items like this from New Year's, 1891, when the Moores entertained at an open house for the last time before moving to Warm Springs Avenue:

"At her pleasant home on Grove Street, Mrs. C.W. Moore received from 4 until 7. She was assisted by the Misses Moore, Miss Hasbrouck, Miss Horrie, Miss Newman, and Mrs. Calvin Cobb. During the afternoon over one hundred people called, among them being his excellency the Governor and many other prominent citizens of Boise and neighboring towns. Mrs. Moore is a charming hostess and the ladies who assisted vied with each other in extending warm greetings of the New Year.

"In the large dining room a dainty collation was spread, the board being gracefully presided over by Mrs. Moore and her daughters. Although the reception hours were announced to be from 4 until 7, the callers were loath to depart, and it was not until late in the evening that the spacious parlors of the residence were deserted."

27.
Christopher W. Moore.

28.
The Moore house was pictured in Elliott's 1884 history.

29.
When built in 1879 the C.W. Moore mansion at Eighth and Grove Streets was easily the grandest in Idaho Territory. Its mansard roof was a stylish novelty in Boise City.

Most present Boiseans remember the big mansard-roofed brick house near the corner of Eighth and Grove streets called the DeLamar Apartments. It was demolished by urban renewal in 1971 after strenuous efforts to preserve it as a landmark of the city's history.

Although many remember the building, very few have much of an idea of where the name came from, or of its early history.

The mansion was built by banker Christopher W. Moore in 1879. It was long considered the grandest house in Idaho territory. Its mansard roof was the first example of that French style seen here, and the Moores spared no expense to make it a showplace. A solid walnut staircase and other millwork were ordered from the midwest.

When the Moores decided to build a new house on Warm Springs Avenue in 1891 they sold the Grove Street mansion to Captain J.R. DeLamar, a Belgian-born mining millionaire who awed little Boise City with his wealth, influence, and energy.

Oral tradition has it that DeLamar bought the Moore place as a home for the woman he hoped to make Mrs. DeLamar, but that she turned him down. Permeal French, then a school teacher at Silver City, and later State Superintendent of Public Instruction and Dean of Women at the University of Idaho, so the story goes, was DeLamar's intended.

In any case, although he bought the house, the Captain never lived there. He invested in other Boise real estate in 1891 and 1892, and became a good friend and business associate of Mayor James A. Pinney. In May of 1892 DeLamar leased the house, with option to purchase, to the Arid Club. An open house in the new location was held May 28, 1892.

In September, the glamorous DeLamar was the subject of "a flowing tribute to Idaho's mining millionaire" in the pages of the Statesman. "One of the delights of the Newport season has been the yachting party held by Captain DeLamar on his yacht the 'Fleetwing'," read the account, and said proudly that he was popular in a circle that included the Astors, Vanderbilts and Morgans.

Back in Idaho in October, DeLamar said he might build a home in Boise, and that his other choice was Newport. He actually decided on New York City, and began to sell off his local real estate.

In June, 1894, the Captain visited the city with his bride and her mother. She was Nellie Sands of New York. When he sued her for divorce in 1898, newspaper accounts noted that she was "famous for her indiscretions."

In February, 1894 the Arid Club rented the DeLamar mansion to a Mrs. Bradford who opened a boarding house there. "This building is one of the finest in the city, with large and elegant rooms. The house

30.
Captain J.R. DeLamar cut a glamorous figure in little Boise City.

31.
The DeLamar was a Basque boarding house for half a century. It looked like this in the 1950s.

32.
The DeLamar's elegant brackets were saved by the Idaho Historical Society when the house was demolished in 1971.

warming was greatly enjoyed by her guests. After dinner (they) retired to the parlor and were charmingly entertained by the ladies with music."

W.E. Pierce & Co. bought the property in 1904, and it continued to be a boarding house for another 66 years. During most of this time its residents were Basque sheep herders. Many a tale could be told of convivial meals around the big dining room table, of hearty Basque cooking, and of a "home away from home" for lonely young men from Spain.

The square-towered Eastlake-style house of Mr. and Mrs. J.W. Daniels at 14th and Bannock Streets was one of Boise City's most striking homes of the 1890s and also one of its most cultured.

John William Daniels was superintendent of Boise schools for more than 20 years and a man of remarkable cultural attainments and education. He could, if needed, teach Greek, Latin, French, German, Geology and Astronomy, in addition to all branches of English and Mathematics. Mrs. Daniels was well known as a teacher of piano, giving lessons to Boise children in the beautiful Daniels home.

When the house was finished in the spring of 1888, The Statesman said, "We do not agree with some who think it too fanciful. It is not plain by any means — but the style is carried out with such perfection throughout all its appointments as to give it a unique appearance. The tower adds to its beauty. They are becoming quite common in the prevailing architecture of the east."

Although the Daniels tower was one of Boise's first, there would be dozens more in the next few years. The popular notion that "a man's home is his castle" achieved expression in houses that were towered to look like castles.

The Daniels lawn, flowers and shrubbery also received notice in the newspapers. The meticulous care "the professor" gave to everything he touched was generally admired, sometimes envied, and occasionally criticized. In his scholarly pursuit of excellence the English-born teacher and administrator was bound to appear too perfectionist to some parents and school board members.

Widely praised for his dedication as a teacher and disciplinarian, he nevertheless antagonized many adults by appearing to be an arrogant martinet, but an admirer called him "the ablest disciplinarian of the West" and said, "What is remarkable about his discipline is that he rules by love and not by force." The same observer rather fulsomely noted that "Mr. Daniels is to education what Napoleon was to war."

Daniels had war aplenty in his stormy career as administrator of Boise's public schools. He was generally supported by The Idaho Statesman for the remarkable progress the city's schools had made under his leadership. Central School, a mansard-roofed brick building of imposing size and style was built early in Daniels' tenure. It stood on the site of the senate wing of the present state capitol.

An anti-Daniels faction was active in the 1890s, seeking election of school board members who would turn him out. The Statesman alternately supported the Superintendent or his detractors during this period. In September, 1894, it supported anti-Daniels candidates who would see that "this presumptious dictator will dictate no more," but a few years later joined leading citizens in defending him against new attacks.

33.
School Superintendent J.W. Daniels' elegant house was notable for its Eastlake styling and rich ornamentation.

34.
Central School was built during Superintendent Daniels' reign. Children lined up like little soldiers for this "Napoleon of education."

33

The school board elections of 1899 and 1900 were heated. Mayor Moses Alexander broke a tie vote of the board in 1899, keeping Daniels in office. In 1900 a near-tragedy sobered both factions in the emotional issues growing out of Daniels' leadership. H.C. Branstetter of the antis and H.B. Eastman of the pros scuffled on the steps of city hall. Branstetter drew a revolver and fired at Eastman in the midst of a crowd of people. The bullet passed between the legs of former mayor James A. Pinney and ricocheted away, miraculously without hitting anybody.

Boise lost the devotion and talents of Mr. and Mrs. J.W. Daniels when he was finally let go by the school board in 1903. They had touched the lives of hundreds of children who would become the city's leaders and had done much to make Boise a cultural oasis in the sagebrush plains of Idaho.

34

The Richard C. Adelmann house at 221 West Jefferson Street was not a mansion, but in most ways it was a typical Boise dwelling of the 19th Century. Old photographs of the city suggest that people of average means lived much as the Adelmanns did — in wooden framed houses with small rooms and no conveniences.

Since insulation was poor or non-existent, and heating was supplied by wood or coal stoves, small rooms could be snug and practical in winter. Few Boise homes had indoor plumbing until the 1890s, making the unpleasant daily chore of emptying and scouring chamber pots a part of life. Water had to be pumped and carried, and heated on a stove, even in summer on wash days or bath days. To iron clothes, sad irons also had to be heated on a stove at all seasons. Nearly all of the work fell to the women, and it was back-breakingly hard. For some Boise families in the 1870s and 1880s a Chinese cook or house servant relieved them of part of this physical burden, but most could not afford it.

If daily chores in the Adelmann household were fairly typical of Boise in the 19th Century, the Adelmanns themselves were not. Richard C. Adelmann had come to New York from Germany with his parents when only eight years old. At eleven he lost his mother, and at fifteen ran away from home to enlist in the Union army in the Civil War. From 1862 until 1865 he was in nearly every major campaign until severely wounded and given his discharge from service.

In July, 1872 Adelmann arrived in Boise with an aunt and uncle, Mr. and Mrs. William Jaumann. Shortly after his uncle opened a saloon on Main Street, young Richard opened his own Gem Saloon. It was one of the city's popular hangouts for a generation.

Boise had a large German community, and Richard made many friends. One of the families he met was that of Charles Ostner, a German-born frontier artist of considerable talent who had achieved local fame by carving a life-size statue of George Washington on horseback and presenting it to the people of Idaho in 1869. Ostner had two attractive daughters, Emma and Julia, and Richard Adelmann would marry them both.

Emma Ostner was married to Richard on July 11, 1875. Sons Alfred and Carl, later well-known Boise business men, were born of this union. After the birth of her second child Emma succumbed to an illness from which she never recovered. In 1882 Richard married her sister Julia. They had four children, William, John, Warren and Julia.

Almost from the beginning of his Boise career Dick Adelmann was a popular member of the volunteer fire company. He was often elected to office in the organization and served as chief more than once. When the volunteers disbanded in 1902 in favor of a professional fire department, they continued to have annual reunions at which pioneers like Adelmann were honored. Early photos show the white-

35.
Richard C. Adelmann, Civil War veteran, saloon-keeper, volunteer fireman, and miner.

36.
The Adelmann house at Third and Jefferson as it looked shortly before its relocation to Julia Davis Park.

37.
Dick Adelmann and family at his mine east of Boise City, 1902. Father-in-law Charles Ostner is at left with Julia Ostner Adelmann.

36

bearded Civil War veteran in his fireman's uniform leading the parade.

Son William Adelmann later spoke of his father's lifelong obsession with mining: "Father put a lot more money into the Idaho earth than he ever took out of it." In 1899 the City Directory listed Richard C. Adelmann as a miner, and family photos show him at work in his mine near Aldape summit on the old road from Boise to Idaho City.

About 1912 Richard Adelmann lost his sight as a result of old head injuries received in the Civil War. Veteran firemen serenaded him every year on his birthday at the little house at Third and Jefferson Streets. He died in 1933 at age 87, a venerated pioneer of Idaho.

The Adelmann house was moved to the Idaho Historical Society's Pioneer Village in Julia Davis Park in 1981.

37

38

Peter and Mary Sonna's fine brick house on Ninth Street near Front was filled with lilting feminine voices during most of the years the family lived there. The Sonnas had daughters Annie, Amelia, Mary and Agatha before son Peter, Jr. was born in 1879. Daughter Laurina was born soon after. Mary Sonna was a native of Austria. She married Peter Sonna in 1870 when she was 20 and he was 35.

New Yorker Sonna had earlier come west looking for gold, as had so many other Boise pioneers. He tried California first and then followed the new rush to Idaho in 1860. He lived briefly in Orofino, Lewiston, and Warrens Diggins before coming to Boise Basin in 1862. He arrived in Boise City in 1863, year of the town's founding, and set up one of its earliest general merchandise businesses.

Although general stores carried everything from groceries and clothing to blasting powder, Peter Sonna decided to specialize in hardware and mining supplies. Like many another ex-miner, Sonna made his fortune supplying the camps rather than pursuing the elusive gold of the mountain streams.

In the 1870s Peter and Mary decided to take their young daughters back to New York. They sold the business and crossed the country, only to return two years later when the new owner failed. In order to protect his investment, Peter Sonna had to stay in the hardware business whether he wanted to or not. He never left Boise again, and became one of its most successful and respected leaders.

1888 was a big year in Sonna's career. He built the finest commercial block in the city at 9th and Main, with his hardware store on the first floor and an opera house upstairs. The dedication in December drew visitors from all over southern Idaho. The railroad offered half-fare tickets and ran extra trains from Mountain Home and Huntington, Oregon. Attorney General R. Z. Johnson delivered the dedicatory oration.

In the early Nineties Sonna began building westward from the opera house, eventually acquiring the old Presbyterian Church building at Tenth which he sold to the builders of the Idanha Hotel. Throughout his business career it was a matter of pride to Peter Sonna that he "never borrowed a dollar" to carry out his own projects, even though he had been vice president of the First National Bank of Idaho since 1876, and in the lending business.

In 1890 Sonna was one of the promoters of the new east end hot water system. In 1893 he was elected mayor and sold the hardware business he had operated for nearly 30 years. As mayor Sonna was noted for generosity and support of civic improvements. He often paid for them out of his own pocket. Noteworthy examples include the covered reservoir he built for Boise Barracks to encourage the army to continue the post, repairs to the Cottonwood Creek flume, and the purchase of uniforms for the police force. (The reservoir is still there.)

38.
Peter Sonna, mayor, capitalist, merchant, and philanthropist, was devoted to his city.

39.
The Sonna house on Ninth Street was a substantial brick hipped-roof structure with dormers. Family members posed near its neat picket fence.

40.
Mary Sonna was born in Austria.

39

The Sonna girls were sent East to school, but the house on Ninth Street continued to be the scene of lively social gatherings during vacation months. Mrs. Sonna often entertained her circle of women friends with luncheons and parties.

It was Peter Sonna's custom to take Mary for a buggy ride around the city every morning after breakfast. He did it as usual on July 9, 1907, the day he died.

40

Judge Henry E. Prickett and his wife Martha built what was described in 1884 as "the most stylish, and probably the most expensive residence in the city." The house was begun in May, 1883, and the Pricketts moved in on January 16, 1884. It stood on the corner of Main Street and Third, across from the United States Assay office.

Although Boise had resisted having a city government for four years, the fact that townspeople could not get clear title to their real estate until the city was chartered led to action in 1867. Henry E. Prickett agreed to serve as Boise's first mayor when the candidate elected refused to take office. (For this reason, all chains of title in the original townsite go back to 1867 and contain Prickett's name.) In 1868 Prickett chose not to run for mayor, but a pro-charter candidate was elected and city government has continued without interruption ever since.

Henry Prickett practiced law in Boise City for many years. His newspaper ads promised "collections made and promptly remitted; conveyance done with neatness and dispatch; claims against the government prosecuted; and having had large experience in public land matters, he will promptly attend to all business with the U.S. Land offices for homestead and pre-emption claimants." The English-born attorney later served as a justice in the Idaho Supreme Court.

Being mayor of Boise City was not regarded as much of an honor in the early days. When Judge Prickett died in Hailey on June 14, 1885, his obituary in the Idaho Tri-weekly Statesman did not mention the fact that he had been the first to hold the office.

Later owners of the elaborately dormered mansard roof house at Third and Main included George Ainslie and James H. Hawley. They, like Prickett, were lawyers who also held political office.

George and Sarah Ainslie lived in the richly ornamented house at Third and Main from the early 1890s until the turn of the century. As a young attorney he had come to North Idaho in 1862. From 1869 until 1873 he edited the Idaho World at Idaho City. In 1875 he was elected District Attorney and served until 1879 when elected to Congress. Ainslie was a founder and president of the Boise Rapid Transit Company which, in 1891, began running Idaho's first electric streetcars east on Main Street past his home.

James H. Hawley acquired the house in 1908. The famed attorney had been mayor in 1902-03 and would be elected Governor of Idaho in 1910. The Hawleys, who were married in Quartzburg on the 4th of July, 1875, had six children: sons Edgar T., Jess B., James H. Jr., Harry R., and daughters Emma and Elizabeth.

Hawley was probably involved in more murder cases than any lawyer in American history. A notable effort of the kind was his defense of Diamondfield Jack Davis, accused of killing two Cassia County sheepherders in 1896. Hawley was also the prosecutor in hundreds of cases, including that of Big Bill Haywood in 1906. After his death in 1929, son James H. Hawley, Jr. lived there until 1936.

41.
Boise City's first mayor built this elegant mansard roofed house in 1883. It was the home of prominent lawyers for half a century.

42.
George Ainslie served in congress and edited The Idaho World *before founding the street car company.*

43.
Boise Rapid Transit Co. street cars began running past the Prickett-Ainslie-Hawley house in 1891.

44.
James H. Hawley was one of Idaho's greatest attorneys. He became Mayor of Boise and Governor of Idaho.

41

42

43

44

Arthur D. Foote was one of the ablest and most visionary engineers who ever toiled in the West. But his petite wife Mary was more famous than he, both in their lifetime and since.

Mary Hallock Foote was an artist and writer who managed to publish her work regularly in national magazines while living in an isolated lava rock house in a canyon ten miles east of Boise City. She also raised a family under conditions that were primitive and challenging beyond anything she had known as a girl in the east.

When Wallace Stegner wrote his Pulitzer prize-winning novel, *Angle of Repose,* about the Footes and their life together, he made Boiseans and thousands of readers across the country aware of one of the truly remarkable women the city has known. Although the novelist took artistic liberties, the main facts of the story are close.

Arthur and Mary Foote had lived in the mining camp of Leadville, Colorado before coming to Boise. Here, he envisioned a great canal that would draw water from Boise River as it comes out of the mountains and send it to irrigate thousands of acres on the benchlands of the valley. What is today lush green farmland and tree shaded suburbs was nothing but miles of sagebrush desert when Foote planned the New York Canal. Although he devoted a dozen years of his life to the project, and was well-known and respected in Boise, Arthur Foote lived with frustration and disappointment. The money needed to complete the canal was not forthcoming and he was finally forced to move his family to California.

The Footes had two homes in Boise — the first the unusual "Canyon House" Arthur designed and built in 1885 at the bend of Boise River just south of today's Lucky Peak dam. The second was a farmhouse near present Hillcrest Country Club (memorialized only by Foote Street nearby).

The Canyon House was considered both a novelty and a showplace by Boiseans. Although Stegner's book makes much of the loneliness and cultural isolation Mary felt while living there, evidence suggests that there was plenty of company and that the Footes were active in Boise society. For one thing, Mary's sister Elizabeth and her husband John Sherman also lived in Boise during those years, and the Footes and Shermans were often mentioned in the columns of the Idaho Statesman as part of what was quaintly labeled "Society's Dizzy Whirl." Their circle of friends included the Eoffs, the Shoups, the Nugents, the Ainslies, the Perraults, the Branstetters, Professor and Mrs. Pasmore, and the Simonses.

"On Tuesday evening Mr. and Mrs. Eoff entertained their friends with progressive euchre," read a May, 1892, item. "The favors were extremely pretty . . . consolation prizes were awarded to Mrs. Foote and Mrs. Richardson . . .". As an active charter member of the Woman's Columbian Club, Mary would have known most of Boise's social elite. She was appointed to the club's fund-raising committee to

45.
Mary Hallock Foote, heroine of Wallace Stegner's Pulitzer Prize winning Angle of Repose.

46.
The Canyon House stood near present Lucky Peak Dam.

47.
This Mary Hallock Foote illustration appeared in Century *magazine in 1888. The verandah of Canyon House was its setting.*

46

see that the Idaho building at the Chicago Fair of 1893 was properly furnished and a credit to the new state.

When son Arthur, Jr. sought appointment to the U.S. Naval Academy in June, 1892, he was attending prestigious St. Paul's School in Concord, New Hampshire, second only to Phillips Exeter as the most distinguished in the state. The Statesman said that his application was backed by some of the "best citizens" of Idaho.

The Canyon House, with its two-foot thick lava rock walls and wide shady verandahs was excellently designed for its site. It is the setting for a number of Mary Hallock Foote's illustrations, made to accompany stories published in *Century, Scribners,* and other magazines. She also used Boise scenes, such as an 1889 full-page illustration in *Century* which showed a young mother with her baby in her arms in Lafayette Cartee's Grove Street orchard.

Only the foundation of Canyon House remains today. After standing empty for many years it gradually decayed and then was burned. Most of the stones were hauled away.

47

Julia Davis Park is one of Boise's most popular places. Its verdant acres follow the river from Capitol Boulevard on the west to Broadway Avenue on the east, making an attractive setting for the Idaho Historical Museum, Boise Gallery of Art, the city zoo, band shell, rose gardens and a variety of recreational facilities.

Who was Julia Davis? Boiseans first heard of her in April, 1871, when the Idaho Tri-weekly Statesman announced her marriage to Thomas Jefferson Davis. The groom and his brother were among the seven men who met in the Davis' log cabin on July 7, 1863 to lay out the Boise City townsite. The bride was Miss Julia McCrum of Galt, Ontario, Canada.

Since Tom Davis was one of the young community's best known bachelors, as well as one of its founders, The Statesman could not resist headlining the story of the wedding "Another Veteran Gone." It joined the community in wishing the newlyweds happiness. When Julia returned from a visit to the eastern states in February, 1874, the paper noted the young couple's reunion by saying, "Tom is happy again."

Tom Davis and his brother Frank got their start in Boise Valley in 1863 when they homesteaded 360 acres of government land. They raised potatoes, onions and cabbage that first season — a crop they sold in the booming mining towns of Boise Basin for $50,000. In 1864 Tom Davis imported young fruit trees at $1.25 each and started southern Idaho's horticultural industry. By 1874 he was prosperous enough to court Julia and get married. At summer's end the Davis orchards contained 6000 trees — several kinds of apples, pears, plums, apricots, peaches and cherries.

Profitable crops of hay were raised on other Davis land for sale to stage companies and to the mining camps. Tom eventually acquired more than 1000 acres in or near the city — the basis of a fortune in real estate, even if the orchards had not continued to produce.

As the turn of the century neared, Tom, Julia and the Davis orchards had grown old together and were ready for retirement. Although they had lost their firstborn son on his fourth birthday in 1876, six other children had grown to maturity and would live long lives. There was time to enjoy a pet deer which played in a fenced enclosure behind the Davis house on Seventh Street (now Capitol Boulevard), and for Tom to join in founding a chess club. He was elected its first president.

In 1899 Tom and Julia Davis offered the city fathers 30 to 40 acres of river land for development as a park if the city would undertake to care for it and control flood waters which regularly eroded the river bank. The matter was referred to committee. It was years before the city felt able to accept the gift, but arrangements were completed just before the death of Julia Davis on September 19, 1907. Thomas Jefferson Davis died on June 10, 1908 with the knowledge that the park would be named for his beloved wife.

48.
Tom and Julia Davis built this fine house on what is now Capitol Boulevard.

49.
Thomas Jefferson Davis.

50.
Julia McCrum Davis.

48

49

50

Christopher W. Moore, his wife Catherine, and their six children moved into the big brick house on Warm Springs Avenue at Walnut in February, 1892. The Statesman described it as "unpressed brick with a tendency to the Queen Anne style." There were ten bedrooms, electric lights and, most remarkable of all, natural hot water heat.

Banker Moore was a founder and president of the Boise Artesian Hot and Cold Water Co. that was soon supplying much of the east end and part of downtown with geothermal heat. The Moore mansion was the nation's first dwelling so heated. The Statesman observed a phenonemon that would be familiar to Boiseans in the years after: "The hot water . . . causes the ground surrounding the subterranean pipes to become dry and baked. A few feet from the region of the pipes, at the present time, the earth is frozen and covered with ice and snow."

Christopher Moore's parents had moved their family across Idaho in a covered wagon in 1852 bound for Oregon. Young Chris was seventeen at the time. In 1862 he returned to Idaho, lured by the gold discoveries that brought thousands of men into the mountains on foot or on horseback. Like other argonauts, Moore soon found that there was more money to be made in business than in mining. He became associated with B.M. DuRell in a firm that supplied many of a mining camp's basic needs: banking, assaying, general merchandise and fast freight. Branches were set up in Ruby City, Idaho City, and Boise. In 1867, with other incorporators, they established the First National Bank of Idaho. For most of the next half century Moore was its president.

Catherine Minear, a native of Virginia, married Chris Moore on July 3, 1865. Their six children were Alice, Laura, Crawford, Anna, Marion and Raymond. Alice married Dr. H.S. Bettis in 1894. Laura married J.W. Cunningham in 1898, and it was she who inherited the Warm Springs mansion and lived there until her death at age 94 in 1963. Marion Moore moved to Australia, but the other children spent most of their lives in Boise.

Laura Moore Cunningham was born in Boise in 1869 when the town was only six years old. She was one of its most influential women throughout her long life, and at her death was characterized by community leaders in remarkably similar words: "A truly great lady — she lived for others." "Gracious, lovely, a great lady." Mayor Shellworth called her "a great lady of the old school." The Statesman said Mrs. Cunningham was "one of the last exponents of the gracious way of social life that flourished in Boise from the turn of the century . . .".

51.
Still the biggest house on Warm Springs Avenue, the Moore-Cunningham mansion at the corner of Walnut Street is one of the city's acknowledged landmarks. In 1892, when this picture was taken, its trees and shrubs had just been planted.

51

John and Laura Cunningham had no children of their own, but their big house was the scene of family gatherings long remembered by nieces and nephews. Aunt Laura did everything with style. Garden parties, to which hundreds were invited to aid one of Laura Cunningham's "causes," were memorable as well. She was on the board of the Children's Home Society for over thirty years and a valued supporter of Boise Junior College from its beginnings in 1932.

J.W. Cunningham also lived a long life. When he died in 1946 at 88 he had lived in Boise for 66 years. With W.H. Ridenbaugh he organized the city's first electric light company in 1887 and was a director of Idaho Power Co. from its formation in 1908. He was also vice president of his father-in-law's bank for nearly forty years.

Mary Blackinger and Hosea B. Eastman were married 20 years before they had a house of their own. That is because H.B. was a hotel keeper, first at Silver City and then in Boise.

Episcopal Bishop Daniel S. Tuttle officiated at the couple's wedding in Silver City in 1872, where Hosea and his brother Ben ran the Idaho Hotel. In 1877 the Eastmans bought Boise City's pioneer Overland House, an 1866 landmark at Eighth and Main that was still the capital city's finest hostelry.

Benjamin M. "Manse" Eastman remained a bachelor all his life, but was so much a part of his brother's family that he came with them in 1892 when they moved into their first (and last) home on Warm Springs Avenue.

The Eastman brothers started west in 1862. Like many pioneers of that time they took the sea route by way of Panama to California. They drove a 30-mule freight team from San Francisco to Canyon City, Oregon, before eventually reaching Silver City.

Silver City had two principal hotels in the Sixties — the Idaho, which the Eastmans bought, and the War Eagle, run by Valentine and Margaret Blackinger. The Blackingers were natives of Bavaria who had recently moved to Idaho from New York with their five children. Two more were born in Silver City. Mary Ann, the oldest, was 22 when she married H.B. Eastman in 1872. The Blackingers moved to Boise soon after the Eastmans did, and the families were closely associated thereafter. Three of Mary Blackinger's sisters also married prominent Boiseans: Timothy Regan, M.A. Regan, and John D. Springer.

Mary Eastman's two sons were both born in the Overland House, Frank M. in May, 1878, and Ben S. in July, 1880. New Hampshire native H.B. Eastman sent his boys to Phillips Andover Academy and then to Yale. He maintained a lifelong pride in his Yankee heritage. When Boise City's New England Association was formed in October, 1897, H.B. Eastman was enthusiastically elected its first president.

The Idaho boys did well at Yale, and when the DeLamar gun club challenged the Boise club to a shooting match in the summer of 1899, Frank and Ben were on the Boise team. "Frank made himself famous by winning the intercollegiate match for Yale," noted the Statesman. When the Eastman boys returned to school in September that year, their father went along to be the yachting guest of mining millionaire J.R. DeLamar during the New York celebrations accompanying the return of Admiral George Dewey, "hero of Manila Bay" in the Spanish war just ended.

H.B. Eastman was prominent in Boise business and banking all his life. He built the Overland (later Eastman) Building at Eighth and Main in 1905 on the site of the old Overland House. He was president of the Pacific National Bank of Boise and a founder of the Boise City National Bank. He was general manager of the Boise Artesian Hot and Cold Water Co. which built the Natatorium, and

52.
Mary and Hosea Eastman's big house on Warm Springs Avenue was the only one they ever had. Before building it in 1891-92 they had always lived in hotels. The Eastman house was destroyed by fire in 1956.

53.
Architect John C. Paulsen designed the great Boise Natatorium for H.B. Eastman the same year he did his house.

52

vice president of the Eastman-Teller Hardware Co. Mary Blackinger Eastman was a charter member of the Woman's Columbian Club and prominent in social and charitable activities.

When H.B. Eastman brought Helena architect John C. Paulsen to the city to design a Natatorium for the hot water company in 1891, he also commissioned his own mansion at 1215 Warm Springs Avenue. Ground was broken in September and the house was built of pressed brick brought from St. Louis. A picture of the 26 room mansion appeared in the Statesman on July 31, 1892 and the family moved in in September. The house was destroyed by fire on February 17, 1956, in a tragedy that took the life of Mrs. Ben S. Eastman, widow of H.B. and Mary's second son who had died in 1945.

53

The last great house to give Grove Street special distinction was the towered Queen Anne mansion that Franklin and Irene Coffin built in 1892. Although Grove had been the city's finest residential thoroughfare in the 1870s, it was gradually supplanted in the Nineties by Warm Springs Avenue and Harrison Boulevard. The Coffin house was as imposing as the best built elsewhere, and much closer to downtown.

Few pioneers enjoyed being one as much as Frank Coffin. Throughout his life he loved to recall his youthful adventures and to keep alive old friendships with those he had met on the frontier. Mrs. Coffin was also a pioneer, and joined her husband in hosting several memorable banquets and reunions for old timers.

As newlyweds, Frank and Irene Coffin had taken the long and arduous journey from Portland to Boise City in 1873 by stagecoach. Although Frank had knocked about the mining camps of Idaho since 1862, it was both a trial and an adventure for a young woman from the midwest.

Like nearly all of Idaho's early settlers, Frank Coffin had come in search of gold. However, it was the tinsmith trade he had learned in Kansas that turned out to be the foundation of his fortune. He did sheet metal work in both California and Oregon between expeditions to the gold fields, but in 1866 settled down in Boise City working as a tinner for George H. Twitchell. In 1873, the year of his marriage, he bought out his employer and began the development of the largest hardware and sheet metal business in Idaho Territory.

With his younger brother Sherman he opened branch stores in Hailey and Caldwell — new railroad towns built by the Oregon Short Line in the early eighties. As Idaho's agricultural economy grew The Coffin Brothers stocked every kind of machine farmers needed — reapers, mowers, binders and hay derricks. They also carried stoves, pumps, ice cream freezers and milk pans.

Irene and Franklin Coffin raised three daughters, Irene, Henrietta and Elma, and one son, Craig. Irene and Elma married Boise business men. Henrietta married Lucius Holbrook, a dashing young army officer who served in the Philippines in the Spanish war and became a general in the First World War. Boiseans followed with interest the military career of this young man and claimed him as their own after he married the fair Henrietta.

The Coffin photo albums record life at the big house at 1019 Grove street during years when the daughters were courting, and later when they brought husbands and grandchildren to visit Irene and Frank. Son Craig worked as a teller in the Boise City National Bank where his father was president for many years.

54.
Frank and Irene Coffin were distinguished pioneers of Boise City.

55.
The Coffin mansion on Grove Street was the last great house built on the city's pioneer residential thoroughfare.

55

The Coffin mansion was the scene of some of Boise's most elegant entertaining. Its towered Queen Anne style, spacious porches and rich ornament made it one of the dwellings always pointed out to visitors. It was the living symbol of an American dream — that a young man or woman could rise to wealth and social respectability through their own efforts in the new lands of the West.

James H. Bush married Ellen Kelly in January, 1876. She was the 28-year-old daughter of Judge Milton Kelly, editor and publisher of the Idaho Tri-weekly Statesman. He was a rising young man in the community with a lifetime of adventure behind him at age 32.

56.
The Bush house on Franklin Street was (and is) one of the city's fine specimens of Victorian architecture.

57.
Central Hotel, James H. Bush, proprietor.

Only two years before James and Ellen were wed he had purchased one of Boise City's pioneer institutions, a hotel at Seventh and Idaho streets known as Hart's Exchange. (City Hall occupies the corner today.) The big wooden hotel dated from 1866 and had been used by Idaho territorial legislatures for many of their early sessions. Bush renamed it Central Hotel.

Before settling down to married life and a business career in Idaho's capital city, Jim Bush had been a miner in Boise Basin. He had gone first to the Pacific coast via Panama in February, 1865. He arrived at Placerville, Idaho in April, having walked all the way from Umatilla Landing on the Columbia river. The 1870 census takers found him at Placerville on August 3, and recorded a net worth of $4500 — a substantial amount in 1870, suggesting that Bush was an energetic and ambitious young man. His purchase of one of Boise's leading hotels four years later confirms this.

There are a number of indications in the records that have come down to us that Jim Bush was a typical "macho man" of the frontier. Lovers of the John Wayne image would find Bush to be their kind of western pioneer.

In 1881 father-in-law Milton Kelly, printed this tribute to Bush's manhood: "On Monday evening an immense specimen of humanity, evidently laden with a heavy cargo of bug juice, went around town spoiling for a fight. The last man he ran across was Bush, of the Central Hotel, who laid him on the portico of the hotel, and Marshal Paxton coming that way shortly afterward, took him to the cooler for repairs. On Tuesday it would have been difficult to discover whether the prisoner had disputed the right of way with a locomotive, collided into a harvesting machine, or been run through a thresher. Anyway, he had found the man he was looking for."

If James H. Bush emerges as something less than a hero in this episode, he is not untypical of our pioneers. They had fought hard and risked much to achieve a stake in the new West. No man could impose upon them or their property, without a scrap.

Kelly of the Statesman frequently plugged improvements at the Central Hotel and noted in 1876 that "to judge by the crowd that goes in and out the interior must be furnishing all that is needed."

Throughout the 1880s, with his family growing, Bush engaged in other enterprises besides the hotel. He ran mule teams to Kelton, Utah, hauling supplies from the Union Pacific railroad before the Oregon Short Line was built across Idaho. He also found time to be active in the city's volunteer fire company, and was elected foreman of Boise Engine Company Number One in 1882.

In sound financial condition by 1890, when Idaho became a state, the Bush family joined in a local building boom that produced dozens of fine new houses for the city's pioneer businessmen. In September, 1891, the Statesman announced that a fine brick residence was planned for the corner of Eleventh and Franklin streets at a cost of $6000. When it was completed in 1892, the paper noted that "visitors to the city say that Mr. Bush's residence compares favorably in point of architectural beauty with houses of many wealthy men in large eastern cities."

That same summer Bush was elected first president of a driving association "for men interested in fast horses." The Bushes were often seen out for a Sunday spin in their handsome carriage with a matched team of high-steppers. They were the envy of all.

If ever a Boise residence deserved to be called a showplace it was the palatial towered mansion of Will and Mary Ridenbaugh. "The Mills," as it was known, had the usual Queen Anne styling, featuring complicated shapes, many porches, and fancy cut-shingled surfaces. It was unique in having not one but three picturesque towers.

The site was as striking as the house, on landscaped terraces facing Boise Avenue, just below the bench south of the city. "The Mills" took its name from the pioneer flour and lumber mill that had operated nearby since 1865. The Isaacs brothers ran it until 1874 when it was taken over, first by the Grangers, and then by William B. Morris.

Will Ridenbaugh came to Idaho in 1872 to work for Morris, who was his uncle. In addition to running the mill, Morris was superintendant of the Northwest Stage Co., and interested in the reclamation of desert lands by irrigation. He began an ambitious canal building project in 1877, but died suddenly in 1878 leaving Ridenbaugh as manager of the estate and its interests.

The year he took charge of his uncle's holdings, Will also took a wife. Mary Elizabeth Black was one of the five daughters of Mr. and Mrs. Charles Black of Missouri. The family had come to Idaho in 1864, settling first with other Civil War refugees in a community near later Caldwell they named Dixie. (Black and six of his brothers had served in the Confederate army.) By 1864 thousands of people from the border states had fled the dislocations and dangers of the war to start life anew in the far West.

Black moved his family to a ranch and stage station 15 miles east of Boise City in 1866. It was soon known as Blacks Creek station, famous for hospitality, good cooking, and the beauty of the five Black girls.

Mary Elizabeth was sent to St. Michael's parish school in Boise and later to St. Vincent's academy in Walla Walla. She taught school for several terms before her marriage to Will Ridenbaugh, and maintained a strong interest in education throughout her life.

While living in the modest house which preceded the 1891 building of their mansion, Will and Mary became widely known and admired — he for his enterprise as a business man and she for her leadership in cultural affairs. Ridenbaugh completed the canal which still bears his name, developed a 2000 acre wheat farm on the bench (now covered with houses) and was a founder and partner in the first electric company, a lumber company, and the Natatorium company.

Mary Ridenbaugh loved gardening. It was said that she personally set out every tree and shrub at The Mills after the new house was built, and that her landscaping skills inspired many other Boiseans to attempt similar beautification projects.

A charter member of the Columbian Club, she took a leading part in many of its projects, including chairing the building committee which

58.
Mary Black Ridenbaugh had beauty, brains, and money — an unbeatable combination.

59.
The Mills was a masterpiece of the towered Queen Anne style. Its landscaped grounds and unusual setting gave it special distinction.

59

erected and funded the 1925 clubhouse, and founding Boise's Carnegie library. She served as a Regent of the University of Idaho for many years and secured a women's dormitory building later named Ridenbaugh Hall.

In March, 1892, architects Campbell & Hodgson unveiled the plans of a new North End house for Thomas and Caroline Logan. They described it in detail for readers of the Idaho Statesman:

"Ascending broad steps we land on a large piazza ten feet wide. Crossing this we obtain entrance through large doors into a paneled vestibule. By moving one of the panels a closet is exposed. Passing through the vestibule we arrive at a large hall 14 x 14 with a large open fireplace under the stairs, which are five feet wide.

"This hall contains a number of little nooks and seats. The finish in this room is of oak. Turning to the left we enter truly a beautiful room, 28 feet long, at the end of which is a semicircular window, taking in the entire end of the room. This is the dining room, and is finished in quartered oak, with a buffet, etc. Adjoining this room are the china pantries, a model convenience, the shelves of which are enclosed and of glass. Next we come to the butter pantry, then to the kitchen, which is finished in natural Norway pine. The house will be heated by hot air, and the plumbing will be made a special feature."

Curiously, this description makes no mention of one of the house's prominent features. The large front parlor has a handsome fireplace with a round-arched stained glass window over the mantel. The account also omits any reference to the living quarters upstairs.

The Logans' first Boise residence (described on page 12) was the red adobe house in the Pioneer Village in Julia Davis Park, occupied by the family for a quarter century. Sadly, Mr. and Mrs. Logan were not able to enjoy their new mansion very long. They had barely moved in when the pioneer merchant and four-time mayor fell ill. In February, 1894, the Logans went to California for his health, thinking they might have to stay a year. He died on a train near Shoshone on May 28, 1894, on a return trip to Boise.

Son Leonard Logan, who was two years old when he arrived in his parents' covered wagon from Wisconsin in 1864, was an established business man himself at the time of his father's death. At the turn of the century he moved his own family into the big house with his widowed mother. She died on May 16, 1908.

Leonard and Grace Coffin Logan had three daughters: Helen (Mrs. Irving W. Hart, Jr.), Carolyn (Mrs. Reuel Smith), and Catherine (Mrs. Richard Price).

Like his father, Leonard Logan was a "Capitalist," and was so listed in city directories. In addition to Logan & Walker, "exclusive boot & shoe dealers," he had interests in mines, real estate, and cattle. Most of these holdings were inherited from his pioneer father. At his death in

60.
Caroline Logan came to Boise by covered wagon in 1864. Her baby girl died on Camas Prairie when the Logans were 100 miles short of their destination.

61.
Thomas E. Logan did not live to enjoy the beautiful house he built on North Eleventh Street in 1892.

September, 1929, the papers noted that he had spent a lot of his youthful years as a cowboy, herding his father's cattle. He had also attended business school, preparing to take over the family interests.

The impressive house at 1205 North 11th Street, built by Thomas E. Logan and long occupied by his son's family, is now the home of Ron and Betsy Twilegar. Leonard Logan, like Ron Twilegar, served on Boise's City Council.

62

William E. Borah came to be known as the "Lion of Idaho" during his long and distinguished service in the United States Senate (1907–1940). His skill at oratory was legendary. It is said that when word passed through the corridors of the U.S. Capitol "Borah's up!", there was a mad rush to get into the Senate chamber to hear him, whatever his subject.

As a young attorney newly arrived in Boise City he had also attracted attention and admiration. Although his first year was a hard one and clients few, people gradually began to realize that this was no ordinary young man. As a Fourth of July orator he made a fine impression. As a lawyer he showed himself eloquent, shrewd and resourceful.

Borah became involved in local Republican politics soon after his arrival in late 1890. He worked for the election of William J. McConnell to the governorship in 1892 and 1894, and served him as part-time secretary. McConnell was a successful business man in Moscow, Idaho at the time of his election. Because Mrs. McConnell stayed in North Idaho due to poor health, the new governor brought his petite and vivacious blond daughter Mary to the capital with him. She and Borah saw each other often as they worked in her father's campaigns.

In 1895 Borah and "Mamie" McConnell were married in the parlor of Cyrus Jacobs' little house at 607 Grove Street. (Governor McConnell and Cy Jacobs had been close friends for over 30 years). Since Borah had legal business to attend to in Caldwell, the happy couple went there by train for the honeymoon. Caldwell's brass band serenaded them outside their hotel.

Bill and Mamie bought the only home they would ever have in Idaho when they acquired the romantic "gingerbread house" of Walter E. Pierce at 10th and Franklin. Architect Tourtellotte labeled it a "cottage" on the plans he drew up in 1891, but it was a large and complex structure with towers, turrets, porches, and elegant decoration.

Mrs. Borah was a popular addition to Boise's social circles and she loved to entertain. Borah, by now making a name for himself, and swamped with work, had large offices downtown at 8th and Main in the new Pioneer Block. He fitted up one of the spacious rooms in the new house as an office and study. The walls were lined with books.

One anecdote, recalled in McKenna's biography of Borah, relates that he came home to find the house full of Mamie's friends playing cards. He greeted them, then ducked quickly into his study. When he emerged much later the guests had all gone home. Mamie commented, "Bill, if you hadn't been so loquacious they might have left sooner."

The oral history collection at the Idaho Historical Society contains a delightful tape of Mrs. Borah, made when she was 99 years old, in which she tells stories of Bill Borah's courtship 75 years earlier.

The Pierce-Borah house was moved to a site in the valley west of Garden City in the 1950s when Boise High School expansion threatened it with demolition.

62.
William Edgar Borah was Idaho's most noted political figure of the 20th century.

63.
The Pierce-Borah house was moved to a site west of Garden City in the 1950s.

64.
Mamie McConnell Borah was known in Washington society as "Little Borah". Always considered "frail," she lived to be 104.

65.
Governor James H. Brady bought the mansion at 120 Main Street from Victoria Louise Eoff in 1908.

66.
The Eoff house was labeled "Neo-Gothic" when completed in 1898 from plans by John E. Tourtellotte. Flat Tudor arches on its porches are its only remotely Gothic feature.

Victoria Louise Eoff had few rivals as the acknowledged leader of Boise's club and social life in the 47 years she lived here. She and her banker husband Alfred E. Eoff built one of the city's grandest houses at the corner of Second and Main in 1897-98. Its $10,000 cost made it one of the most expensive residences in the city at the time.

Mrs. Eoff was born Victoria Louise Marsh in Brighton, Ontario, Canada on January 30, 1859. Orphaned young, she went to live with a married sister in San Francisco. She married Alfred E. Eoff there in October, 1881. He had also lost his mother while in his teens and had gone west in 1861 to the Pike's Peak gold rush in Colorado. There he joined Col. George Shoup's volunteer regiment to fight in the Civil War. (Shoup also came to Idaho after the war and became the new state's first governor in 1890).

After an adventurous life as agent for Ben Holliday and Wells Fargo stage companies in a variety of frontier outposts, Alfred worked his way from bookkeeper to assistant cashier to cashier in the Wells Fargo bank in San Francisco. It was there that he met and married Victoria Marsh. He organized The First National Bank of Prescott, Arizona in 1884 and came to Boise in March, 1886, to found The Boise City National Bank.

From the day she arrived in Boise Victoria Eoff was a leader in every kind of good work that would benefit her new home town. She was a founder of the Woman's Columbian Club, of the Idaho Children's Home and of St. Luke's Hospital. Social custom of the day favored regular "at homes" when Victoria Eoff and her friends received callers. There were also formal dinners and whist parties that included their husbands.

An invitation to the Eoff's spendid residence at 140 Main was cherished by all who had social ambitions. The house itself was a showplace, described by The Statesman in 1899 as "palatial". The hall, dining room, and sitting room were finished in oak and the parlor in cherry. Each mantelpiece was of a different design and wood. "The house is fitted with all the modern conveniences," said The Statesman, "and the result of a great deal of study." John E. Tourtellotte, Boise's leading architect of the period, was its designer.

When Alfred Eoff died suddenly in June, 1908, the city went into mourning. "No man had more friends . . . few can hope to have as many," read The Statesman obituary. He was hailed for his steady leadership and generosity in public affairs. His widow sold the big three-story house in December, 1908 to newly-elected Governor James H. Brady of Pocatello. Brady was a bachelor and wanted a suitable mansion in which to entertain during his term of office.

Victoria Eoff continued to take an active lead in the community's social and benevolent activities until her death in June, 1933. "Mrs. Eoff's home was a synonym for hospitality, and even in these days when formal calls appear to be out of date, it was her pleasure to call upon newcomers and to invite them to visit her." The Eoff tradition of hospitality at 140 Main is continued today by Romaine Galey Hon. The house is listed in The National Register of Historic Places.

Moses and Helena Alexander built the big house at the corner of Third and State Streets in 1897, the year the German-born clothing merchant was elected mayor of Boise City for the first of two terms. Alexander would go on to make national political history by becoming the first Jewish governor the country ever had.

Both of the Alexanders were born in Germany and emigrated to the United States in their teens, Moses from Bavaria and Helena from Saxony. They were married in St. Joseph, Missouri on November 5, 1876.

Soon after his arrival in New York in 1868 young Moses Alexander went to Chillicothe, Missouri, where he found work as a clerk in a clothing store. In less than five years he was taken into partnership in the business. In 1886 he was elected to the Chillicothe city council, and a year later to the first of two terms as mayor.

On July 16, 1891, Alexander saw Boise City for the first time when he got off an Idaho Central branch line train from Nampa at the old wooden depot on the bench. He took the dusty ride by horse-drawn carriage into the city and began a reconnaissance that led to his decision to locate in Idaho's capital and start another clothing business.

Idaho had become a state just a year earlier, and Alexander found business booming. New buildings were gong up at a rapid rate, and the population would double in little more than a year.

The clothing business Moses Alexander established grew with the city, as did his own popularity. The Alexander name became known throughout southwestern Idaho through billboards advertising "Alexander the One-Price Clothier." An Alexander float appeared in most local parades, and in 1896 the paper reported that he had "several voluminous signs hoisted over his place of business."

With the support of the Idaho Statesman, Alexander was elected mayor in July, 1897, defeating pioneer former mayors Peter Sonna and James A. Pinney by a margin of two to one. The headlines called it a "Great Improvement Victory."

In 1901, when Moses Alexander was re-elected, the family included daughters Emma, 23, Henrietta, 21, and Leha, 16. Son Nathan was 18 and attending school in New York City, preparing for a career in the family business.

A colorful piece of family memorabilia, now on display in the Idaho Historical Museum, is the exotic plaster polychrome statue of Salome presented to Mayor Alexander by the city council when he retired from office in 1903. Members of the family recall that Alexander was never fond of the piece and banished it to a storage shed where it languished for half a century before grandson Nathan Alexander presented it to the museum in 1975.

Moses Alexander was elected governor of Idaho in 1915 and was re-elected in 1917. His clothing business expanded to include stores in

67.
Moses Alexander was an astute politician and reformer as well as an able business man. He was Mayor of Boise and Governor of Idaho.

68.
Helena Alexander, like her husband, was born in Germany.

69.
The Alexander house at Third and State Streets was built by local carpenters from plans in a newspaper. It has been acquired by the State of Idaho and restored as a memorial to America's first Jewish governor.

69

Weiser, Caldwell, Nampa, and Baker and Ontario, Oregon. Son Nathan operated the Baker store in the 1920s and took over the chain after his father's death in 1932.

In 1926 friends and relatives gathered in the State Street mansion to help Moses and Helena celebrate their golden wedding anniversary. Letters and telegrams of congratulation came from all over the country.

The house passed from Moses to Nathan to Nathan, Jr., who sold the historic structure to the State of Idaho in 1977. It has been home to the Idaho Commission on the Arts since that time. It is listed in the National Register of Historic Places for its architectural distinction as well as for its association with one of Idaho's most distinguished business and political figures.

The Warm Springs Avenue mansion built by Nathan and Rosa Falk in 1901 was torn down in 1970. Its golden oak dining room was carefully dismantled by volunteers and later skillfully restored and installed in the Idaho Historical Museum by curator William G. Dougall. The Idaho Historical Auxiliary helped with furnishings to bring the elegant room back to its original appearance.

The Falk house was a handsome addition to the series of fine homes built by pioneer Boise business men along the Avenue after the streetcar line and Natatorium were begun in 1891. Like a number of others it was designed in the Queen Anne shingled style by John E. Tourtellotte, and featured a corner tower and wrap-around verandah.

Nathan Falk, like his brothers David and Sigmund, was born in Germany. The Falks were among Boise City's first merchants, establishing their Main street general store near the corner of Eighth in 1868. They also had a branch in Payette valley for a generation which gave its name to a neighborhood and a post office called Falks Store.

The firm was known as D. Falk & Brother until 1881 when older brother David retired to follow other business interests — in particular, mining in the new Wood River district near Ketchum and Hailey. It was Nathan Falk & Brother from that time until reorganized in 1891 as Falk-Block Mercantile Co., and in 1900 was the Falk Mercantile Co., but Nathan remained its president.

In 1878 Nathan went back to Germany and returned with a bride. She was Rosa Steinmeier, ten years younger than he. In 1880, when their first daughter Bella was seven months old, Rosa's 17 year old brother Julius came from Germany to live with them and clerk in the store's grocery department. The young couple also had a teen-age hired girl at this time to help take care of the baby. The Falks would always have servants, in later years as many as five.

Nathan Falk was popular in Boise's business community. In 1876 he was elected president of a newly organized Occidental Club, and in 1890 was a charter member and first treasurer of the Arid Club. In the 19th Century Boise's Jewish merchants regularly observed the holy days of the faith by closing their stores. The Idaho Statesman, from its earliest issues, took respectful notice of this custom and ran articles explaining the traditions of Judaism.

Few citizens in all of Boise's history have enjoyed the universal affection and respect that Nathan Falk did. When he died unexpectedly in July, 1903, it was a shock felt by the whole community. The city's leaders lavished praise on a man who had devoted a lifetime to improving his city through generous contributions and service in every worthy cause.

70.
The Nathan Falk house was a gracious example of Queen Anne styling.

71.
The Falk mansion's oak-paneled dining room was removed from the house just before its demolition in 1970. It can be seen today in the Idaho Historical Museum.

72.
Nathan and Rosa Falk's family posed for this portrait in 1898.

Nathan Falk enjoyed the beautiful new home he had built for his family at 139 Warm Springs Avenue for only two years before he died. His widow Rosa survived him another 37 years, and lived to see her sons and daughters grow into respected members of the community, devoted to its welfare as their father had been.

Bella married Stanley Smith and her sister Anne married Samuel Rothchild. The sons were Leo J., Ralph, Harry and Theodore. Leo J. Falk became a prominent Boise business leader and Ralph a well-known doctor.

Preservation is a movement in American history whose time has come. Like all such ideas there were critical moments when the balance of public sentiment shifted almost imperceptibly from indifference to new commitment. For Boise, such a moment came in 1974 when a small group of citizens organized to preserve and restore the Bishops' House, then scheduled for demolition. We can all be grateful that they succeeded in a task that many regarded at the time as an impossible dream.

In 1889 the Episcopal Church built a wooden frame rectory for its bishops at the corner of Second and Idaho Streets. The church had bought the entire block bounded by First and Second, Idaho and Bannock, as a site for St. Margaret's School, a large brick building completed east of the rectory in 1892. The church had earlier established a strong educational tradition with academic courses taught in a wing of the 1866 St. Michael's Church (now preserved on the Boise State University campus, but without the school addition).

The Bishops' House of 1889 was a modest two-story building designed by James King, the city's first trained architect. It cost $2700. When plans were made in the late 1890s for a new rectory next door to St. Michael's, the Second and Idaho house was sold to Bishop James B. Funsten. In 1899 the church decided to build a parish hall next to the cathedral instead, and to greatly enlarge and improve Bishop Funsten's residence.

John E. Tourtellotte was employed as the architect of the remodeling project. His plan called for an impressive three-story tower at the southeast corner, a second story porch above the entry, and large verandahs on all four sides of the building. The Queen Anne style, which Tourtellotte had helped popularize in Boise with many other houses in the decade, featured fancy cut-shingles and a complex sculptural form. There was a big third floor attic and a rectangular hip-roofed pavilion at the southwest corner. The main tower and this pavilion were topped with sheet metal finials in the form of religious symbols used since the Middle Ages — crosses in circles and crosses and hearts.

The foundation and first floor were made of sandstone blocks with rough faces, beautifully fitted and joined.

Six Episcopal bishops lived in the house at 120 West Idaho: J. B. Funsten, 1899-1918; Frank Hale Touret, 1919-24; Middleton S. Barnwell, 1926-35; Frederick E. Bartlett, 1935-42; Frank Rhea, 1942-57, and Norman Foote, 1957-60. In 1964 Bishop Rhea Center was incorporated to provide office space for social agencies and to accommodate senior citizen activities of various kinds.

73.
The Bishops' House moved down Warm Springs Avenue in November, 1975, en route to its new site near the Old Idaho Penitentiary.

74.
The Bishops' House and St. Margaret's School as they looked early in the century from the corner of Second and Idaho Streets.

75.
Friends of the Bishops' House, a non-profit corporation, now maintains the historic landmark for the benefit of the community. It is a popular setting for weddings, receptions and parties.

74

On June 7, 1974, St. Luke's Hospital announced plans to demolish the house within 90 days to build a parking lot as part of its expansion in the neighborhood. People who cared about the big old house organized for action. Today the 220 ton Bishops' House stands 2½ miles away on Old Penitentiary Road, beautifully restored, the scene of festive social activities throughout the year.

75

76.
John Haines, pioneer realtor, was elected Mayor of Boise and Governor of Idaho.

77.
The Haines house still stands at Tenth and Hays Streets, lovingly restored to its original beauty.

78.
Governor Haines in front of W.E. Pierce & Co. at Tenth and Main Streets.

The big house at 919 West Hays Street, like every other older dwelling in the city, has a story to tell. Like its neighbors, it was the scene of personal successes and failures, of joys and sorrows, of good times and bad.

John and Mary Haines must have seemed the very models of success and happiness to their Boise friends. They had wealth, social position, and statewide prominence. When they began their new home at the corner of 10th and Hays Streets in August, 1904, widespread local interest in the progress of its construction was reflected in a series of newspaper items.

John Haines had come to Boise in 1890 as a member of the firm of W. E. Pierce & Co., pioneer realtors. He and L. H. Cox had joined Pierce in Kansas shortly before the move west. Only close friends knew that Kansas was a painful and bitter memory for John and Mary Haines, and that they, even more than Pierce or Cox, had an emotional need to start a fresh life in Idaho.

J. D. Flenner, a pioneer Idaho newspaper man, came to know John and Mary Haines well. His is the only account we have of the early years of their marriage. Mary Symons was the daughter of Quaker parents. Her father was a minister of that faith. John Haines' father was also a Quaker. The young couple (he was twenty) were married in Lynnville, Iowa in May, 1883. They bought coach tickets on the railroad for as far as their money would take them. After a short time in Nebraska, where John clerked in a bank, they moved to Kansas.

"Mr. and Mrs. Haines were pathfinders of Kansas," wrote Flenner. "They went out on a claim, built a house, cultivated the land and did pioneer work. They enjoyed themselves fine out there and had great times. They had one of the very best teams in the state, one of the choicest cows, a fine dog and other pets. A beautiful baby girl was born to them there and she was the light of the home. But the dread shadow came and she folded her little hands and crossed over to the company of the immortals and left them bowed and stricken with a grief that lingers still."

John Haines, who "got his early education by plowing corn in the summer time and shucking it out of the snow in the winter, poring over his books at night by the light of the candle," was a great success in the real estate business in Boise. He made a wide circle of friends, was active in politics, and got elected mayor of the city in April, 1907.

In 1912 he was elected Governor of Idaho. His re-election in 1914 was frustrated by a scandal not of his making. The State Treasurer was jailed on the eve of the election for embezzling large sums of state money. Moses Alexander, the Democratic candidate, won the election.

When John Haines died at home on June 4, 1917, after a long illness, a friend said sadly, "He wanted to give the people of Idaho a good administration. He wanted it to be clean and above reproach. He wanted it to be the crowning work of his life, and the failure to realize his dreams broke his heart and hastened his death."

Timothy Regan and Hosea Eastman had a lot in common, despite different backgrounds. Regan's parents had come to America from Ireland. Eastman's parents were New England Yankees whose forebears had been here for generations.

Both young men arrived in Silver City soon after the Owyhee mining camp was established in 1863. Both married daughters of Valentine and Margaret Blackinger, Bavarian-born proprietors of the War Eagle Hotel. Eastman and his brother Manse ran the rival Idaho Hotel, and when Tim Regan bought a half-interest in it in 1875 the Silver City hotel trade was all in the family. Tim's brother, Phil, joined the combine in 1877.

That year the Eastmans moved to Boise City and bought the Overland House. The Regans ran the Idaho Hotel until 1889 when they too moved to the capital city. The Blackingers had already arrived, and in a short time the Boise hotel scene was also a family affair. Tim Regan and Frank Blackinger ran the Capitol Hotel and the Eastmans ran the Overland. Tim, by now a rich man from mining investments, bought School Superintendent J. W. Daniels' elegant Bannock Street house.

Family ties were strengthened still further in 1892 when M. A. Regan, a nephew, married Lillie Blackinger in the Timothy Regan home. She was the younger sister of Rose Regan and Mary Eastman. The Blackingers, Regans and Eastmans made up a large extended family, insuring big parties indeed on holidays and special occasions.

At the turn of the century Tim and Rose Regan and sons John and Will were living in the Capitol Hotel. Brother-in-law Frank Blackinger was the manager. By 1900 most of the city's wealthy pioneers had built mansions on Grove Street or on Warm Springs Avenue. The Regans built theirs in 1906 at 110 Main. It was a choice location, not far from downtown, on the street car line that ran out Warm Springs to the Natatorium, and next door to Alfred and Victoria Eoff's house, one of the city's showplaces.

Colonial architecture was the latest thing, and architect John Tourtellotte and his partner C. F. Hummel were masters of the popular new style. The Statesman described the Regan house on December 30, 1906: "colonial style; cut stone; hot water heat, water color interior decorations; hardwood finish; modern baths, halls and drawing rooms; billiard room, recreation room, etc." (The "watercolor decorations" were rediscovered 70 years later when owner Robert Bushnell, Jr. removed layers of wallpaper that had covered them for a generation. The "watercolors" were actually frescoes — paintings on wet plaster that become part of the wall when dry rather than just surface decoration.)

A feature of the Regan house is its exceptionally fine woodwork. The hall and front parlor are golden oak. An adjoining parlor is birdseye maple, and the handsome dining room is solid red cherry.

Timothy and Rose had more than their share of personal tragedy. Daughter Lillie and son Harold died young. John Regan was killed in

79.
Timothy Regan made his fortune in mining and banking after years in the hotel business.

80.
The Regan dining room is made of solid cherry wood. The classical china cupboard is especially handsome.

81.
John Regan died in action in France in World War I.

80

action in France on August 4, 1918. It was widely believed by friends and relatives that the sorrow of losing his son hastened the death of Timothy Regan on October 7, 1919. He was survived by his wife and son Will Regan.

John Regan Post Number Two of the American Legion of Idaho is named in honor of Tim and Rose's son. Will Regan was a community leader who built another of the city's outstanding residences. The house at 1009 Warm Springs Avenue was the only Mission style house in the city when completed in 1911. The Statesman called it "a gem."

81

82.
The L.H. Cox house was another of the handsome Colonial revival residences designed by John E. Tourtellotte and Company early in this century. The order was Ionic.

In April, 1906, the Idaho Statesman announced that L. H. Cox, a prominent Boise realtor, was planning to build a fashionable Colonial style mansion on Warm Springs Avenue. When Cox let the contract in July a detailed description appeared:

"Mr. Cox is of the opinion that he has one of the choicest sites for a residence in the city. It is in a grove of walnut trees. The residence will rank with the finer homes of the city when it is completed. The plans, which were drawn by Tourtellotte & Co., are for a colonial structure. It will have 10 rooms and will be modern in every way. There will be two commodious porches supported by large pillars."

The house was complete in December. In a year-end summary of building for 1906 the cost was listed as $12,000. Hot water heat, used on the Avenue since 1892, was not unusual, but "sanitary plumbing" was still enough of a luxury in Boise that it received special mention.

The Cox house at 1308 Warm Springs Avenue was one of several important Colonial style dwellings designed by the Tourtellotte firm at the beginning of the century. (Timothy Regan's at 110 Main, also completed in 1906, was made of stone and cost $17,000).

L. H. Cox and his wife Emma came to Boise City in 1890 as part of the real estate firm of W. E. Pierce & Co. John M. Haines, another partner in the business and later governor of Idaho, was a lifelong friend, dating back to Cox's boyhood in Grinnell, Iowa, when he had worked for Haines' father on the family farm. After a brief course in business college Cox went back to work for the senior Haines.

When L. H. Cox and Emma Ballard married in 1876 they moved to North Dakota where he again farmed. His opportunity for a business career came when old friend Haines invited him to come to Richfield, Kansas, where he and W. E. Pierce had gone into real estate. In Kansas Cox opened a farm implement business and was appointed postmaster.

When Pierce, Haines, and Cox decided to set up a real estate office in Boise in 1890 Cox was made vice president of the firm. Since they were the city's first full-time real estate developers and promoters they revolutionized the business. Idaho had just become a state when the partners arrived and Boise, the capital, was booming. W. E. Pierce & Co. sold more real estate than all of their competitors combined.

Lindley and Emma Cox raised a son, W. Clyde, and two daughters, Mamie and Lyda. The son joined his father's business. Mr. and Mrs. Cox were active members of the Boise Country Club, where he was an avid golfer. On June 17, 1923, while on his way to play a round, he was in a minor accident and bumped his head. Although the injury was not considered serious at the time, a hemorrhage followed a few days later. L. H. Cox was 66 when he died.

82

Probably no Boise leader ever built or lived in more fine houses than Walter E. Pierce. Old-timers agree that it was he who established the city's first real estate office upon his arrival from Kansas in 1890. As partners he brought with him John M. Haines and L. H. Cox, also prominent Boiseans in the years that followed.

"In 1890 there was nothing to the town north of State Street," recalled Samuel H. Hays in 1909. "Resseguie, Brumback, and other additions were nothing but farms . . . such a thing as a real estate office was unheard of in Boise at that time and I very well remember that the average citizen believed that the (Pierce) firm would shut up shop within 90 days."

How wrong they were. W. E. Pierce & Co. not only developed one successful north end addition after another but built a series of major downtown commercial structures as well. Of those still standing the Idaho Building, 1912, and the IB&T Center (Hotel Boise, 1930) are the most significant.

Pierce and his first wife Georgie were a popular addition to the city's social circles. The community's leaders recognized and appreciated the contributions to Boise's growth and prosperity the energetic Pierce and his partners were making. When the firm published 5000 plats of the city for mailing to prospective investors outside Idaho in 1895, the Statesman said "The enterprising firm deserves no little credit for the trouble they have been to", advertising Boise. With the newspaper's support, W. E. Pierce was elected mayor in 1896.

Georgie and Walter Pierce separated in 1913. The divorce settlement reflected his success since coming to Idaho. Mrs. Pierce received the handsome home at First and Idaho, the couple's electric automobile, $100,000 in stock in the company, and an additional $100,000 to be paid in annual instalments over 10 years.

In 1914 Walter E. Pierce built the big house at 1805 North 21st Street (now the Governor's Mansion) for his second wife, Maude Evans. She was a Pennsylvania girl who had graduated from nursing school in Chicago before coming to Idaho. After losing a son, Walter Jr., in 1916, the couple raised two daughters, Helen Elizabeth and Margaret.

From 1923 until 1943 the Pierces lived at 1201 Harrison Boulevard. In 1948 they moved into the Hotel Boise which he had built in 1930. Walter E. Pierce died in August, 1951. Mrs. Pierce lived until 1966.

83.
Walter E. Pierce was Idaho's pioneer real estate promoter. He, more than any other person, built Boise between 1890 and 1930.

84.
Idaho's "Governor's Mansion" is really a big bungalow. Walter E. Pierce built it in 1914 for his new bride, Maude Evans Pierce.

84

Boise's architecture for over a century has been the product of local builders and architects. Only a few of the city's outstanding dwellings were designed by out-of-state architects, and even fewer by people considered "names" in the profession.

Kirtland K. Cutter of Spokane was one of the Pacific Northwest's most talented and successful designers. His fame spread throughout the region, leading to commissions in several states. Cutter planned two houses for prominent Boise business leaders, both of which grace Warm Springs Avenue today.

Leo J. Falk, son of pioneer merchant Nathan Falk, commissioned Cutter to design a home for him, his wife, Helen, and their three children in 1922. The striking tile-roofed stuccoed house at 1320 Warm Springs Avenue anticipated the Mission Revival that blossomed in Boise after the new Union Pacific depot was built in that style two years later.

Cutter, who also designed the English half-timbered C.C. Anderson house in 1925, was noted for his ability to work in virtually every popular architectural style. His own house in Spokane was a Swiss chalet. For Spokane's wealthiest families he provided plans of Colonial, Mission, half-timbered and Italian Renaissance mansions — no two alike but all elegant and richly ornamented.

Leo J. Falk was born in Boise in 1882, oldest son of Nathan and Rosa Steinmeier Falk. After education in Boise and California schools he went to work in the family mercantile company, eventually succeeding to its presidency. In February, 1914, he married Helen Friendly of Elmira, New York. Their three children were Elaine, later Mrs. Albert Chambers, Jane, who married Arthur Oppenheimer, and Leo J. Falk, Jr. who became a doctor.

Helen Friendly Falk was a civic leader whose influence and active life matched that of her husband. She was a member of the board of directors of every cultural organization in the city: Idaho Historical Society, Boise Gallery of Art and Boise Civic Symphony. She was a charter member of the Junior League of Boise and active in the American Red Cross, United Fund, and polio and cancer foundations.

Leo J. Falk's best-known accomplishments include formation and leadership of the corporation that planned, built and operated the Owyhee Hotel. He also built the Egyptian Theater. Both are Boise landmarks on The National Register of Historic Places, as is his home on Warm Springs Avenue.

85.
Leo J. Falk

86.
Helen Friendly Falk

87.
Spokane's famous architect K.K. Cutter designed this stylish house for Leo and Helen Friendly Falk in 1922. Stuccoed walls continue the motif of the house, creating privacy and outdoor "rooms."

87

Warm Springs Avenue is noted for handsome houses of several styles and eras, set in spacious landscaped grounds. None surpasses the English half-timbered Tudor-style mansion of Columbus C. Anderson at number 929, designed in 1925 by architect Kirtland Cutter of Spokane.

C. C. Anderson came to Boise in April, 1896, and founded the Golden Rule Store. He had learned the retail business in Boulder, Colorado, in a store also called the Golden Rule, and had known a fellow employee in its Longmont, Colorado, branch named J. C. Penney. Both young men shared ideas that would revolutionize department store merchandising and make them great fortunes. In an age when department stores relied heavily on charge account customers and had to do a lot of paper work, Anderson's system was "no credit, no bookkeepers, no stationery, no billheads, and a money-back guarantee." By 1913, when Anderson described his principles in those words, he had stores in Weiser, Payette, Caldwell, Midvale, Mountain Home, New Plymouth, Emmett, and Boise. By 1950 he had a chain of 34 stores.

Anderson was 25 when he married Henrietta Walter of Boise on June 15, 1898. The young couple lived in a modest frame house at the corner of Main Street and Avenue A at first, and then at 145 East Idaho. Although he never had children of his own, C. C. Anderson was active in many local charities which benefitted them. He was president of the Idaho Childrens Home Finding and Aid Society, and a trustee of St. Luke's Hospital.

When he died in December, 1958, it was recalled that he had been especially fond of youngsters and that he had personally handed out treats to 905 of them at his Warm Springs Avenue house on Halloween, 1955. (Obviously, the children knew where to go.) Others remembered years later that he used to toss pennies to the little ones as he walked down the street or encountered them in the aisles of his big store on Idaho Street (now the Bon Marche).

After the Golden Rule stores became affiliated with Allied Stores of New York in 1938, Anderson served as a member of its board of directors for the next 20 years. He was a director of the First National Bank of Idaho for more than 50 years.

In both 1917 and 1941 C. C. Anderson was active in civilian programs to aid the war effort. In the first war he served as State Fuel Director. In the second, he was State Director of the Office of Price Administration. He is also remembered as a lifelong Democrat and a trustee of the First Methodist Church of Boise. The substantial sums he gave and willed to the church made possible completion of the Cathedral of the Rockies.

Like so many others among those who came to Idaho in the 19th Century, Anderson proved that America is the land of opportunity.

88.
C.C. Anderson believed in "no credit, no bookkeepers." It made him a rich man.

89.
K.K. Cutter's second contribution to Boise architecture was the imposing English-style house he designed for Mr. and Mrs. C.C. Anderson in 1925. Cutter was a master eclectic who could handle all styles with grace and effectiveness.

He was born in a log cabin on a farm near Osceola, Missouri, the son of a horse trader. He died 85 years later a rich man with one of his adopted city's finest homes and the reputation for being one of its most generous benefactors.

Mr. and Mrs. William Langroise, who later owned the house, willed it to Boise State University as the future home of its presidents. It is listed in the National Register of Historic Places.

ACKNOWLEDGEMENTS

The people described in this book are among my best friends, even though most of them lived and died before I was born. This personal identification with early Boiseans comes largely from years of reading and indexing the Idaho Statesman from its first issue in 1864, supplemented by voluminous written records in the Idaho Historical Library at Third and State Streets.

I am much indebted to Judith Austin, Guila Ford, Elizabeth Jacox, Larry Jones, Merle Wells and Marjorie Williams — valued colleagues of many years who were unfailingly helpful and patient with my requests. Frieda March of the Idaho Genealogical Library was also of considerable help in running down elusive information. Dee Hart typed most of the manuscript and made valuable suggestions at every stage of the work. Doris Camp also did some of the typing.

Special thanks are due the Idaho Statesman for allowing inclusion of material that first appeared in my weekly Idaho Yesterdays column. I appreciate the editorial assistance of Al Shayt of the Statesman staff over many years, and of Tim Burroughs, my present editor there.

Researching this book also gave me pleasant opportunities to talk with descendants of some of the families represented, to view family photo albums, and to read correspondence. I am especially grateful to Elizabeth Adelmann, Nathan Alexander, Carol Bettis, Frank Holbrook, Peggy Lundy, Jane Oppenheimer, Marilyn Sharp, and Lorene Thurston for supplying me with materials and reminiscences not otherwise available.

Barbara Hansen and Robert Aldridge of Historic Boise, Inc., publishers of this book, gave valuable support to the project, as did Jean Wilson of the Bookshop and Charles Hummel, F.A.I.A.

Arthur A. Hart

INDEX